# 50
# TEACHING
# & LEARNING
# APPROACHES

Sara Miller McCune founded SAGE Publishing in 1965 to support the dissemination of usable knowledge and educate a global community. SAGE publishes more than 1000 journals and over 800 new books each year, spanning a wide range of subject areas. Our growing selection of library products includes archives, data, case studies and video. SAGE remains majority owned by our founder and after her lifetime will become owned by a charitable trust that secures the company's continued independence.

Los Angeles | London | New Delhi | Singapore | Washington DC | Melbourne

# 50

# TEACHING & LEARNING APPROACHES

Simple, easy and effective ways to engage learners and measure their progress

## SHARRON MANSELL

EDITOR
## ANN GRAVELLS

WITH ILLUSTRATIONS BY
### ANDREW HAMPEL

Learning Matters
An imprint of SAGE Publications Ltd
1 Oliver's Yard
55 City Road
London EC1Y 1SP

SAGE Publications Inc.
2455 Teller Road
Thousand Oaks, California 91320

SAGE Publications India Pvt Ltd
B 1/I 1 Mohan Cooperative Industrial Area
Mathura Road
New Delhi 110 044

SAGE Publications Asia-Pacific Pte Ltd
3 Church Street
#10-04 Samsung Hub
Singapore 049483

Editor: Amy Thornton
Senior project editor: Chris Marke
Project management: Deer Park Productions
Marketing manager: Lorna Patkai
Cover design: Wendy Scott
Typeset by: C&M Digitals (P) Ltd, Chennai, India
Printed in the UK

**Library of Congress Control Number: 2019940725**

**British Library Cataloguing in Publication Data**

A catalogue record for this book is available from the
British Library

ISBN 978-1-5264-8876-3
ISBN 978-1-5264-8875-6 (pbk)

At SAGE we take sustainability seriously. Most of our products are printed in the UK using responsibly sourced
papers and boards. When we print overseas we ensure sustainable papers are used as measured by the
Egmont grading system. We undertake an annual audit to monitor our sustainability.

# Contents

# Acknowledgements

I would like to give a special thanks to the following people who have helped me with the production of this book. They have freely given their time, knowledge and advice, which has resulted in some excellent contributions and additions to the content. Without their amazing proofreading skills and honest feedback, this book would not be what it is, and I am truly grateful.

Sarah Gilpin, Head of Teaching, Learning and Assessment at White Rose Beauty Colleges (Harrogate)

Louise C Gulbrandsen QTS Med, Teacher at Loavenstad School

Rick Mills, Technical Training Specialist at United Utilities Water Ltd

Jeminiyi Ogunkoya MSET QTLS, CEO of AASOG UK Ltd

Helen Whittle MSET, QTLS, QTS, English Tutor at White Rose Beauty Colleges

Kelly Woodhouse, Head of Teaching, Learning and Assessment at White Rose Beauty Colleges (Barnsley)

I would like to express a special thank you to my boss, Karen Lee-Cooke, Principal of the White Rose Beauty Colleges, for her words of encouragement and the trust and opportunities she has given me.

I would like to thank Richard, Emma, Steven and Morgan for their continued support and patience.

I would also like to thank my Senior Commissioning Editor (Education) Amy Thornton for her support and guidance.

This book would not have happened without the help and support from my editor Ann Gravells and my illustrator Andrew Hampel. So huge thanks to them.

Every effort has been made to trace the copyright holders and to obtain their permission for the use of copyright material. The publisher, editor and author will gladly receive any information enabling them to rectify any error or omission in subsequent editions.

Sharron Mansell

# Author statement

**Sharron Mansell**

Sharron started delivering education and training programmes on a part-time basis in 1987, before progressing into a full-time career in further education in 2000. She has gained practical work-based skills and a wide and varied understanding of schools' provision, further and higher education, apprenticeships and full-cost courses.

Starting her career as a teacher in a land-based specialist college, she progressed to course management before taking responsibility for several departments within a large further education college. Sharron further developed her knowledge and skills within the sector when her role changed to Head of Services to Business. She is the Assistant Principal of Quality at the White Rose Beauty Colleges and their Ofsted nominee. They are recognised as the UK's largest beauty therapy training provider which was judged Outstanding by Ofsted in 2019.

Sharron is passionate about raising standards in education and is committed to supporting quality improvement at all levels and stages. As well as her work in further education she has also worked with primary and secondary schools as a governor to support quality improvement.

Sharron holds an Honour's Degree in Education and Training, has a Certificate in Education, is a Member of the Society for Education and Training, and holds QTLS status.

**Sharron can be contacted via:**

Facebook: https://www.facebook.com/mansellsharron/

Twitter: https://twitter.com/sharronmansell

LinkedIn: https://www.linkedin.com/in/sharronmansell

Email: sharronmansell@outlook.com

# Editor statement

**Ann Gravells**

Ann has been teaching, assessing and quality assuring in the further education and training sector since 1983. She is a director of her own company *Ann Gravells Ltd*, an educational consultancy based in East Yorkshire. She specialises in teaching, training, assessment and quality assurance.

Ann holds a Master's degree in Educational Management, a PGCE, a Degree in Education, and a City & Guilds Medal of Excellence for teaching. She is a Fellow of the Society for Education and Training, and holds QTLS status.

Ann has been writing and editing textbooks since 2006, which are mainly based on her own experiences as a teacher, and the subsequent education of trainee teachers. She aims to write in plain English to help anyone with their role. She creates resources for teachers and learners such as PowerPoints, online courses, and handouts for the assessment, quality assurance, and teacher training qualifications. These are available via her website: www.anngravells.com

Ann has worked for several awarding organisations producing qualification guidance, policies and procedures, and carrying out the external quality assurance of teaching, assessment and quality assurance qualifications.

She is an Ofqual Assessment Specialist, a consultant to The University of Cambridge's Institute of Continuing Education, and a technical advisor to the awarding organisation Training Qualifications UK (TQUK).

# Illustrator statement

**Andrew Hampel**

Andrew is a designer and lecturer who has been delivering and managing further and higher education art and design courses for 20 years. His design work ranges from traditional watercolour to multimedia video performance pieces.

Outside education, Andrew is a partner in an event company *District 14*, providing marketing and corporate presentations for comic cons.

Having a direct link to the vocational design industry gives his students an excellent opportunity to work directly with his company to provide workshops and materials to the community, along with access to a wide range of professionals including Marvel and BBC Books.

As well as design work, Andrew has a passion for history and is a trustee for a World War Two home front project. He has a special responsibility for educational projects and community outreach.

Andrew has contributed to writing a number of science fiction anthology works and podcasts, as well as writing and illustrating *Quick Histories of Hull*.

Andrew's Online Folio can be seen at: deviantart.com/skaromedia

Andrew can be contacted via email: skaromedia@hotmail.com

# Foreword

If you are looking for innovative, yet easy and effective ways to engage your learners during your sessions, then the chapters in this book are just what you need.

Whether you are new to teaching or are an experienced teacher or trainer, these approaches will give you lots of ideas to help learning to take place in an active way. They might help you to try something different or to adapt what you currently do.

As I worked through the process of editing each chapter, I wished a book like this had been available when I first started teaching. It's fine to read textbooks all about the theory of teaching, but it's putting it into practice that matters, to ensure that learning is taking place.

Sharron has included a few traditional teaching and learning approaches such as *case studies, discussions* and *worksheets,* and added lots of other exciting approaches such as *find your match, hot potato, quescussion, snowballing,* and *true or false.*

Do try out some or all of the approaches, and feel free to adjust them to suit your subject, your learners, and the environment within which learning is taking place.

You will find the Appendix proves useful as it contains lots of ideas regarding how to group your learners for activities.

Both Sharron and I hope you enjoy the book. Please feel free to give us some feedback here: http://www.anngravells.com/anns-books/book-reviews

Coming soon:

> *50 Assessment Approaches*
> *50 Quality Assurance Approaches*

Ann Gravells
www.anngravells.com

# Introduction

## Your role

Your role as a teacher or a trainer gives you the chance to help someone reach their full potential. Great teaching can make a real difference to an individual's life and future employment prospects, whether they are going into their first job, reskilling to have a change in their career, upskilling to go for a promotion, or to take up self-employment. To engage your learners during your sessions you must plan activities which keep their minds active during the learning process. This book will help support you to do just that.

## Using this book

This book is not about theory, it's about giving you some ideas of practical teaching and learning activities to try out. Throughout the book you will find traditional activities that have been recognised as good practice for years, as well as many new approaches. They might not all work, perhaps due to different group dynamics or the maturity of your learners. Or you might try some and then decide to adapt them to suit your own learners' requirements.

The chapters are set out in alphabetical order and you may choose to read the book from start to finish, or to select a title from the contents page to locate a specific activity. Whichever way you choose to use the book, be creative and imaginative, and always check the spelling and punctuation in any handouts given and presentations used. In addition, remember that you should always demonstrate professionalism to your learners to enable them to learn from you and model your behaviour.

## Chapter grids

Each chapter starts with a grid to indicate with a tick whether the activity is suitable for an *individual* learner, a *small group* or a *large group*. It includes the suggested *preparation time*, the *timing* of the activity, and if there is any *after session marking time* required. It specifies the academic *level* the activity could suit, and whether it is *formal* or *informal*, and contains suggestions for the type of assessment, i.e. *formative* or *summative*. The grid also shows the suitability of the activity to encompass and develop knowledge, understanding and skills in *English, maths, digital skills, employability* and *British Values*. If a box in the grid is blank, this means it's not applicable. However, the grid is just a guide and you may feel some aspects will differ for you and your learners.

# British Values

In 2014 the Department of Education published guidance on promoting British Values in schools and colleges to prepare people for a life in modern Britain. Ofsted and the independent inspectorates take the work of schools and colleges in this area into account during their inspections. It's therefore useful if you can embed these whenever possible during your sessions.

The four British Values are:

- democracy
- the rule of law
- individual liberty
- mutual respect for and tolerance of those with different faiths and beliefs.

These values, coupled with the development of employability skills, give a clear message to all learners that they can succeed in life.

# Chapter structure

Each chapter has a series of headings to help you understand how to use the activities:

*What is it?* – An explanation of what the activity is and how to set it up.

*What can it be used for?* – Suggestions of when and where in your session the activity would be most suited.

*Resources* – lists any materials required to undertake the activity. You will need a suitable and appropriate learning environment.

*Advantages* – lists the benefits of using the activity.

*Disadvantages* – lists the difficulties or challenges you may find with the activity.

*How can I measure my learners' progress, meet individual needs and demonstrate stretch and challenge for all?* Explains how you might use the activity to ensure appropriate learning has taken place.

Some of the chapters have specific examples, and at the end of every chapter you will find a handy *tip* and a short list of references for *further reading and weblinks.*

The chapters are illustrated with characters who reflect inclusivity, equality and diversity.

# Using the activities

Many of the activities can be used in succession depending on how long your session is, and the context of the topic or subject. Some of the activities can be used as assessment approaches and be used solely for this purpose, i.e. initial, formative or summative.

A number of the activities can be adapted as icebreakers or team-building activities to develop communication and collaborative skills.

Throughout the chapters you will find activities which require you to group your learners. The Appendix, at the back of the book, gives examples of how you might do this.

All of the activities will enable you to measure the individual progress and stretch and challenge your learners to their full potential. To do this you must know what each learner's starting point is, and any additional learning needs they might have. You should carry out your organisation's initial assessments and skill scans and note these in the individual learning plan (ILP) or other relevant document. If your organisation doesn't have its own initial assessments or skill scans, you could have a go at planning your own questions and devising relevant practical activities. The results of these will help you determine what a learner already knows, understands and can do, in relation to the subject they have chosen to study. Remember to check their current English and maths skills to enable you to support their development in an applied setting or working environment.

The majority of activities are suited to a classroom environment; some are adaptable to the workplace or a realistic working environment (RWE). Others have a blended learning approach which requires learners to undertake homework tasks and to have access to the internet and a computer (or appropriate device).

After the sessions, learners can continue to communicate and learn about the current topic or subject via a learning platform, e.g. Moodle or a virtual learning environment (VLE), by blogging or by using relevant social media platforms.

## Further reading and weblinks

Gov.uk – *Amanda Spielman's speech to the Policy Exchange think tank* – http://tinyurl.com/yaumrt9k

Gov.uk – *Guidance on essential digital skills framework* – http://tinyurl.com/y667pvrb

Gov.uk – *Guidance on promoting British values in schools published* – http://tinyurl.com/m7cw8e7

Gov.uk – *Ofsted raising standards improving lives* – http://tinyurl.com/lczdnn8

ISI – *Independent Schools Inspectorate* – https://www.isi.net

Jobs.ac.uk – *Employability: What are employers looking for?* – http://tinyurl.com/y4dlgz27

# 1 Analogue versus digital

| Individual | √ | Small group | √ | Large group | √ |
|---|---|---|---|---|---|
| Formative | √ | Summative | | Preparation time | Up to 30 minutes |
| Informal | √ | Formal | | Timing | 30-60 minutes |
| British Values | √ | Employability | √ | After session marking? | * |
| English | √ | Maths | * | Digital skills | √ |
| Entry Level | √ | Level 1 and 2 | √ | Level 3 upwards | √ |

*depends upon what and how you are planning to use the approach

## What is it?

Analogue versus digital is about learners finding things out about something from two very different sources:

1.  Analogue – learners do not use anything to do with technology, televisions, radios, phones or electric/electronic devices. They use books, journals and talk to people.

2.  Digital – learners can use technology, televisions, radios, phones or electric/electronic devices. The internet and online sources of information should be encouraged.

Learners should be given a topic to research either individually, in pairs or in small groups (depending upon the size of your group). You will need to decide who will carry out the analogue research (A) and who will carry out the digital research (D). Setting a time limit for the activity will help focus learners' attention. The A learners can then present their findings to the D learners, and vice versa. Depending upon how you have grouped your learners, you might like to decide who will be the presenter.

A discussion can take place as to how easy or difficult the activity was (based on whether the learners were A or D), how their findings compare, and if any information is correct or not. The latter can encourage discussions about what is real or fake, and how research should not totally rely on internet sources.

You will need to have carried out the task yourself in advance, to have an idea of what your learners will find out.

## What can it be used for?

This activity is really useful to show learners how reliance on technology is not always good, e.g. accessing fake information online but believing it to be true. It teaches learners how to use analogue research and enables a discussion on the different techniques which can be used to research something. It also supports learners to develop collaboration skills.

## Resources required

- Relevant textbooks, journals and other paper-based resources (or access to a learning resource centre)
- Electronic devices with internet access

## Advantages

👍 Can be adapted to use as individual, paired work or small groups

👍 Encourages independent thinking and research skills

👍 Can challenge a learner's potential

## Disadvantages

👎 Can be time-consuming to plan

👎 Can be noisy if both sources of research are carried out in the same room

👎 If learners leave the room to research elsewhere, e.g. a learning resource centre, you will need to check they are working safely

# How can I measure my learners' progress, meet individual needs and demonstrate stretch and challenge for all?

Observing how your learners approach the activity, and asking open questions will help you to see how they are progressing. The presentations and discussions at the end of the activity will confirm learners' knowledge and understanding.

Pairing an experienced learner with an inexperienced learner will help to challenge the latter. Alternatively, setting a more difficult subject to research could stretch more able learners higher.

---

### Tip

Depending upon your group size and the time available, you could allocate both A and D research sources to all the learners for the same topic. This would enable them to compare their own findings, rather than with those of the other learners.

---

## Further reading and weblinks

EJLT – *The value of analogue education tools in a digital educational environment* – https://tinyurl.com/y2mo95tm

PolyVision – *Why it shouldn't be analog versus digital in today's classroom* – https://tinyurl.com/y4geehgw

# 2 Bingo

| Individual | | Small group | √ | Large group | √ |
|---|---|---|---|---|---|
| Formative | √ | Summative | | Preparation time | 30 minutes plus |
| Informal | √ | Formal | | Timing | 20–30 minutes |
| British Values | * | Employability | * | After session marking? | |
| English | √ | Maths | * | Digital skills | * |
| Entry Level | √ | Level 1 and 2 | √ | Level 3 upwards | √ |

*depends upon what and how you are planning to use the approach*

## What is it?

Bingo is an activity to encourage learners to match relevant questions to answers, and to understand technical subject words.

Learners start with a blank bingo card (five columns by five rows, 25 boxes in total). They are given a list of 100 technical words (the *answers*) related to the current topic or subject they are working on. The learners must select 25 of the words from the list and copy these into any of the boxes on their bingo grid. Prior to making their selection, learners should be told they must not make any errors when copying the words down, otherwise they will forfeit the game.

You will need to prepare a suitable question or definition for each word on the list you have compiled. This list could be given as a handout or displayed on a screen or board before being removed when the game commences.

Once the learners have prepared their bingo cards you can randomly read out the questions/definitions of the words. For example, a question regarding the topic of Agricultural Livestock would be 'Which breed of cow has the highest milk yield?'. Any learner who has added *Holstein* to their grid can mark it off. 'Which breed of chicken is raised for meat?'. Any learner who has added *Broilers* to their grid can mark it off.

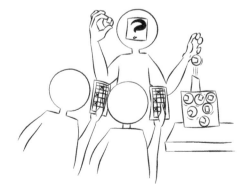

Once a learner has completed a full line (either horizontal, vertical or diagonal) they should shout out 'bingo'. The spelling should be checked and the game continues until someone completes all 25 squares and shouts 'full house'.

# What can it be used for?

This is a fun activity to check learners' knowledge and understanding of technical words. It also supports the spelling of them. Acronyms and jargon could also be included.

Learners could build up a list of these terms over the duration of the course for future reference in their job role. The list could be created via a cloud application or virtual learning environment (VLE) which all learners could contribute to.

# Resources

- Blank bingo cards (or learners can draw their own grid on paper or a suitable electronic device)
- A list of 100 technical words relating to the topic or subject being taught
- 100 questions or definitions for the technical words used

# Advantages

- A fun and effective way of testing knowledge and understanding
- Can be used at any point during the session
- Re-focuses and re-engages individuals
- Can be differentiated to meet individual needs
- It's engaging and supports social learning
- Can make learning fun

# Disadvantages

- Difficult to manage with a large group of learners as it's quite time-consuming
- Learners may become too competitive and disruptive
- Can seem trivial to some learners
- Time-consuming to prepare (but can be used again with other learners)

# How can I measure my learners' progress, meet individual needs and demonstrate stretch and challenge for all?

By identifying the correct word for the question or definition given, learners are able to demonstrate their individual progress. To ensure all learners are stretched and challenged to their full potential, you could randomly select learners to give a definition of one of the technical words. The learner could choose their own word from the grid, or you could select the word for them.

If you have higher level learners, you could split the group into fours. Each learner could devise a shorter list of words with questions/definitions to ask the others in turn.

> **Tip**
>
> If you are working with a very large group you could place the learners in pairs or small groups to work as a team.

# Further reading and weblinks

Teaching Ideas – https://tinyurl.com/ycpxe2jp

Thought Co – https://tinyurl.com/ydblhmdw

# 3  Board rotation

| Individual | | Small group | √ | Large group | √ |
|---|---|---|---|---|---|
| Formative | √ | Summative | | Preparation time | 30 minutes plus |
| Informal | √ | Formal | | Timing | 20–50 minutes |
| British Values | √ | Employability | √ | After session marking? | |
| English | * | Maths | * | Digital skills | * |
| Entry Level | √ | Level 1 and 2 | √ | Level 3 upwards | √ |

*depends upon what and how you are planning to use the approach

## What is it?

Board rotation is an interactive learning activity where different scenarios, questions or instructions are written on a board (or flipchart paper). These are placed around the room for learners to respond to.

You can set up as many boards as you like; usually between five and six is enough depending on the size of your group. Learners are divided into small groups of between four to six, and must work around the room completing the activities written on each board, in rotation.

For example: board 1 could be a question written on flipchart paper which the learners must discuss in their group and add their answer to; board 2 a practical activity; board 3 a problem to solve; board 4 a research activity; and board 5 a worksheet to complete.

In their small groups, learners must identify key learning points and write them on the board before rotating to the next activity. Learners rotate around the room until all the boards have been covered.

Alternatively, you can just use question boards and not have any practical activities. Assign each group to one of the boards and ask them to write their answers under the question before rotating to the next question, where they write their answer below the first answer. Learners continue to rotate around the room until they have completed all of the questions on all of the boards.

At the end of the activity, you should hold a group discussion and ask each learner to identify which board activity they enjoyed the most and why.

## What can it be used for?

Board rotation is an ideal activity to use part way through a topic or subject to amalgamate the learning undertaken so far. It is very interactive and engaging for most learners, as each board requires them to participate in a short activity related to the topic or subject they are learning.

Emphasising respect for each other and the importance of communication will support you in developing learners' knowledge and understanding of British Values and developing employability skills.

Board rotation is also a useful recap activity as it encourages the learners to revisit prior learning.

## Resources

- A room large enough to accommodate the various board activities
- Boards or flipchart paper on which to write the activities
- Pens
- Equipment (if planning practical activities)
- Books or internet (if planning a research activity)

## Advantages

👍 It's engaging and supports social learning and collaboration

👍 Can make learning fun

👍 Allows decision making and problem solving

👍 Demonstrates current skill levels

## Disadvantages

👎 Time-consuming to set up

👎 Learners may become too competitive and disruptive

👎 Some learners may require more processing time to read through the text and comprehend meaning

## How can I measure my learners' progress, meet individual needs and demonstrate stretch and challenge for all?

Observing the groups as they rotate around the boards will enable you to see the learners demonstrating their current skills, knowledge and understanding. Asking the learners to write down their answers to the questions, or their key learning points from each of the activities will support you in measuring their progress. You can also see whether they have made progress from their starting point, and how they react in different situations.

Knowing the learners' starting points and grouping the learners is key to meeting individual needs, e.g. learners of the same ability or level should be in the same groups for this activity to alleviate the higher-level learners giving away the answers. The board questions or activities should vary in level to ensure all learners are stretched and challenged to their full potential.

The group discussion at the end of the activity will also support you in identifying progress, and directed questions could be asked to further stretch and challenge individuals.

## Tip

Ask the learners to write their answers and key learning points on a piece of paper that the other groups can't see, to add stretch and challenge.

# Further reading and weblinks

BookWidgets – *20 interactive teaching activities for in the interactive classroom* – https://tinyurl.com/y82gfon9

Study.com – *What is interactive learning? Overview and tools* – http://tinyurl.com/y5r5jasj

# 4 Brainstorming

| Individual | √ | Small group | √ | Large group | √ |
|---|---|---|---|---|---|
| Formative | √ | Summative | | Preparation time | 10 minutes |
| Informal | √ | Formal | | Timing | 10–60 minutes |
| British Values | √ | Employability | √ | After session marking? | |
| English | √ | Maths | * | Digital skills | * |
| Entry Level | | Level 1 and 2 | √ | Level 3 upwards | √ |

*depends upon what and how you are planning to use the approach*

## What is it?

Brainstorming is a short activity which quickly stimulates learners' thoughts and ideas.

Learners are given ten to fifteen minutes (on their own, in pairs or groups) to list or draw suggestions or ideas related to a topic, subject, theme or problem. This should build on their current knowledge and experience. Learners should be encouraged to think differently and generate as many ideas as they can in the time provided. You will need to plan what will be discussed in advance.

Once learners have completed the activity, a whole group discussion should take place to share thoughts and ideas, and correct any misconceptions.

## What can it be used for?

Brainstorming is a great way for learners to plan a task, where the possibilities for the task are not clearly understood or defined. By noting their thoughts and ideas, learners can share them later with their peers, and select the most appropriate ones to form a comprehensive and achievable plan for the task. You should emphasise how they should respect and embrace each other's opinions. You should also state how good communication will support them in developing their knowledge and understanding of British Values, further developing their employability skills.

It is also an ideal activity for problem solving and team building (if working as a pair or a group) as learners have the autonomy to think freely and generate as many ideas as they like in the time given to solve the problem.

Brainstorming should always lead into another learning activity, e.g. an assignment or a learner presentation.

## Resources

- Paper and pens (or electronic devices) for noting down findings and ideas

## Advantages

👍 Helps learners generate new ideas

👍 Supports learners to communicate ideas and thoughts

👍 Encourages discussion and peer support

👍 Builds confidence, listening and speaking skills

👍 Quick and easy to set up

## Disadvantages

👎 Not all learners may want to take part, and some might need support

👎 Requires learners to be self-motivated

👎 During the group discussion, some learners might be judgemental and overpowering

👎 Less visual or creative learners may struggle to engage with the activity

👎 Learners might digress and not complete within the time limit

## How can I measure my learners' progress, meet individual needs and demonstrate stretch and challenge for all?

Progress measures for brainstorming are difficult as there are no right or wrong answers during the activity. However, to help measure individual progress, ensure you move around the learning environment during the activity, observing and reading each individual's work.

The whole group discussion will support you in identifying and correcting any misconceptions, and allow you to determine learners' starting points prior to progressing to the next activity. In addition, you could ask open directed questions to stretch and challenge particular learners.

Learners can also be asked at the end of the activity to write down one or two key points they have learned. They can state what they will be taking forward into the next activity which will help you meet any future individual needs.

**Tip**

Give learners a verbal prompt by announcing how long they have left to complete the activity, e.g. *You have two minutes left to complete this activity.*

# Further reading and weblinks

Gravells A (2017) *Principles and Practices of Teaching and Training:* Learning Matters/Sage, London.

Petty G (2009) *Evidence-based Teaching: A Practical Approach* (2nd edn): Nelson Thornes, Cheltenham.

ThoughtCo – *How to brainstorm in the classroom* – https://tinyurl.com/ycfjyx5d

# 5 Break it up

| Individual | | Small group | √ | Large group | √ |
|---|---|---|---|---|---|
| Formative | √ | Summative | | Preparation time | 10 minutes |
| Informal | √ | Formal | | Timing | 10–15 minutes |
| British Values | * | Employability | * | After session marking? | |
| English | * | Maths | * | Digital skills | * |
| Entry Level | √ | Level 1 and 2 | √ | Level 3 upwards | √ |

*depends upon what and how you are planning to use the approach*

## What is it?

Break it up is a short activity that breaks away from a whole group activity part way through the session.

Learners will break into smaller groups at some point during the session to discuss a related topic, and then report back to the larger group. The small group discussion should last no longer than ten minutes and the feeding back to the whole group should be no longer than three minutes per group.

## What can it be used for?

Break it up is ideal to use part way through a lecture or a formal session. It allows learners to confirm their learning by discussing the topic/subject in a small group. It also gives them time to discuss and write down key points. This should be shared later with the whole group, demonstrating what they know and understand.

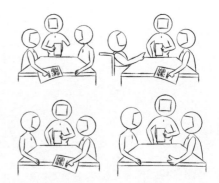

If your group is becoming disengaged, this is a superb activity to re-engage your learners.

## Resources required

*   Paper and pens (or electronic devices) for noting down findings and ideas, or flipchart paper and marker pens

# Advantages

👍 Helps learners to stay focused on a topic/subject

👍 Helps to re-engage, re-energise and re-focus learners

👍 Re-affirms learning

# Disadvantages

🗨 Not all learners might want to engage in this sort of activity

🗨 Discussions must be supervised to ensure learners remain on task

# How can I measure my learners' progress, meet individual needs and demonstrate stretch and challenge for all?

There are two ways to measure progress during this activity. The first is to move from group to group listening and observing the discussion. This will ensure learners are demonstrating their knowledge and understanding of the subject/topic. The second is when the small groups report back key points as part of the whole group activity.

To encourage stretch and challenge, you will need to plan who will be in the small groups prior to the start of the session, rather than letting learners choose their own groups. By planning this way, you will be able to put the more confident verbal learners together, who will naturally stretch and challenge each other. The less confident learners may need a written structure to help them with the discussion, e.g. a question which helps them start the discussion, a question which helps them deepen the discussion, and a question which helps them summarise what they have discussed and identify the key points.

> ### Tip
>
> Allow the learners to develop their own conversation; don't be tempted to ask or answer questions otherwise it becomes teacher led rather than learner led. Any questions learners do have can be asked during the whole group activity.

# Further reading and weblinks

Forsyth Donelson R (2017) *Group Dynamics*: Cengage Learning Ltd, Boston

Preserve Articles – *What is group dynamics?* – https://tinyurl.com/ycajtwcf

# 6    Buzz groups

| Individual | | Small group | √ | Large group | √ |
|---|---|---|---|---|---|
| Formative | √ | Summative | | Preparation time | 10 minutes |
| Informal | √ | Formal | | Timing | 10–20 minutes |
| British Values | √ | Employability | √ | After session marking? | |
| English | √ | Maths | * | Digital skills | * |
| Entry Level | | Level 1 and 2 | √ | Level 3 upwards | √ |

*depends upon what and how you are planning to use the approach*

## What is it?

The buzz group activity is about dividing a group of learners into smaller groups to discuss a question, a particular topic or subject, or to solve a problem.

The buzz groups should be no smaller than three and no larger than six learners. You should prepare a question or devise a problem to give to your learners, which is based on the current topic or subject. This can be the same for all of the buzz groups, or different questions/problems can be used.

Learners should be encouraged to write down key points from the discussion. They should choose a spokesperson within their buzz group who will feedback the findings to the whole group at the end of the activity.

Learners should be given five to ten minutes to hold the discussion simultaneously, followed by feeding back their findings to the whole group.

## What can it be used for?

It can be used to encourage a discussion about a topic or a subject, or to solve a question or a problem you have devised for the learners to resolve. Buzz groups are also a great way to close a session as it enables learners to identify and discuss what they have learned. Using it as a closing activity allows peers to remind each other about particular aspects of the session, thereby learning from each other. Emphasising respect for each other and the importance of communication will support you in developing learners' knowledge and understanding of British Values, and developing employability skills.

# Resources

- A pre-prepared question, topic, subject or a problem for the learners to discuss
- Paper and pens (or electronic devices) for noting down findings and ideas

# Advantages

- Encourages independent thinking skills and problem solving
- Encourages discussion and teamwork
- Builds confidence, listening and speaking skills
- Quick, adaptable and easy to set up
- Can be used to fill in time if necessary

# Disadvantages

- Not all learners may want to take part, and some might need support and/or encouragement to participate
- Some learners may dominate the discussion
- Requires learners to be self-motivated
- Some groups may not be able to reach a conclusion or may digress

# How can I measure my learners' progress, meet individual needs and demonstrate stretch and challenge for all?

There are two ways to measure progress during this activity. The first is for you to move from group to group listening and observing the discussion to check the learners are on track. The second is when the buzz group's spokesperson reports back key points as part of the whole group activity.

To encourage stretch and challenge, you can plan who will be in each of the buzz groups prior to the start of the session, rather than letting learners choose their own groups. By planning this way, you will be able to put the more confident verbal learners together who will naturally stretch and challenge each other. The less confident learners may need a written structure to help them with the discussion, e.g. a question which helps them start the discussion, a question which helps them deepen the discussion, and a question which helps them summarise what they have discussed and identify the key points.

To further develop individuals you could plan who the spokesperson will be rather than letting each group decide.

> **Tip**
>
> Check learners are on task and that they are not having unrelated conversations. Allow the learners to develop their own conversation; don't be tempted to ask or answer questions during their conversation, otherwise it becomes teacher led rather than learner led.

# Further reading and weblinks

Gravells A (2017) *Principles and Practices of Teaching and Training:* Learning Matters/Sage, London.

The Training and Development World – https://tinyurl.com/ybx7xhny

# 7 Card activities

| Individual | √ | Small group | √ | Large group | √ |
|---|---|---|---|---|---|
| Formative | √ | Summative | | Preparation time | 20 minutes plus |
| Informal | √ | Formal | | Timing | 10–20 minutes |
| British Values | * | Employability | * | After session marking? | |
| English | √ | Maths | * | Digital skills | |
| Entry Level | √ | Level 1 and 2 | √ | Level 3 upwards | √ |

*depends upon what and how you are planning to use the approach

## What is it?

Card activities are a way to help learning take place in a fun way, e.g. match, list, order or group items relating to the current topic or subject.

You will need to decide if the activity will be carried out individually, in pairs or small groups. You will also need to give clear instructions and set a time limit for completion. Make sure you de-brief the activity afterwards and state how it relates to the topic or subject. If you don't have any card, you could write on strips of firm paper.

Here are five examples of quick and simple activities using cards; each should be on a separate piece of card:

1. List about 10 separate questions and answers which relate to the current topic. Learners can match the answers to the questions. A discussion can take place if any were matched wrongly.

2. List a few topic headings and related points (e.g. recipes [headings] and ingredients [points]). Learners can list the points under each heading. A discussion can take place as to what is correct or not.

3. List a few actions which need to be carried out in a certain order (e.g. the procedures which must be carried out for a certain process to occur). Learners can then place these in the order they think is correct. A discussion can take place as to what is correct or not.

4. List a few headings with related items which learners need to group together, e.g. different aspects of a particular job role and the tools required for each. Learners need to group the tools according to the jobs. A discussion can take place as to what is correct or not.

5. Write some sentences which are true and some which are false regarding the current topic. Learners need to place them in two columns: true and false. A discussion can take place as to what is correct or not.

# What can it be used for?

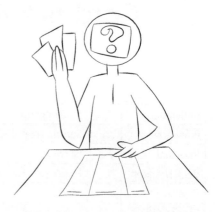

Card activities can be used for a wide range of teaching and learning approaches including: ascertaining a learner's starting point; measuring progress; re-engaging a learner or group of learners; summarising a topic or subject; an icebreaker or extension activities to stretch and challenge individuals.

It takes time to plan, prepare and use the activities, but they will enable your learners to explore the topics in a far more interesting and inspirational way. This can be more engaging than just listening to you talking or watching you demonstrate something.

## Resources

- The card activity (enough for all learners to participate)

## Advantages

- Supports active learning
- Visually stimulating
- Supports memory recall
- Can be fun and engaging
- Great for learners who are usually unwilling to participate in group work

## Disadvantages

- Time-consuming to create and set up (but can be used for future groups)
- Can cause too much competitiveness (if used as a group or paired activity)
- Can seem trivial to some learners
- Some learners may require more processing time to read through the text and comprehend meaning

## How can I measure my learners' progress, meet individual needs and demonstrate stretch and challenge for all?

The card activities should be designed to meet different levels and abilities which will support individuals to demonstrate stretch and challenge, e.g. using activity 1 *question and answer cards*, you could write questions and answers at different levels. The lower level questions could include short questions with closed answers such as *yes* or *no, true* or *false*. The higher-level questions could include open answers where the learner must read the full text to be able to match the correct answer to the question. The latter could be on different coloured card to ensure you use these with the relevant learners.

If you are using the card activity to measure progress, it is important to know each learner's starting point prior to setting the activity, to ensure you are meeting the right level.

---

Tip

If you have access to a laminator when designing and creating the cards, they will become a sustainable resource you can use over and over again.

---

# Further reading and weblinks

Gravells A (2017) *Principles and Practices of Teaching and Training*: Learning Matters/Sage, London.

Kirstens Kaboodle – *Top ten task card activities* – https://tinyurl.com/yb662nvz

# 8 Case study

| Individual | √ | Small group | √ | Large group | √ |
|---|---|---|---|---|---|
| Formative | √ | Summative | √ | Preparation time | 30 minutes plus |
| Informal | √ | Formal | √ | Timing | * |
| British Values | * | Employability | √ | After session marking? | * |
| English | √ | Maths | * | Digital skills | * |
| Entry Level | | Level 1 and 2 | √ | Level 3 upwards | √ |

*depends upon what and how you are planning to use the approach

## What is it?

A case study is an approach which helps learners understand the relevance of a theory or a concept. It can put theory into practice through the use of ideas and examples, which are based around relevant scenarios, hypothetical or actual events.

Using a case study can place the learner in the role of the decision maker, e.g. it can enable the learners to observe different practical ways of doing something. Alternatively you can set a task which your learners carry out to reach a conclusion, or to find a different way of doing something.

The case study is broken down into two stages:

- stage one – the learners read, observe or undertake the activity
- stage two – the learners discuss their ideas and findings.

The case studies you use should be presented to the learners as a problem or an issue which they need to resolve, or for them to select their preferred way of doing something and identify the reasons why.

## What can it be used for?

The case study is ideal when delivering a difficult or emotive scenario, e.g. the political argument for and against euthanasia, or the impact of social media on mental health. It can be used to support practical-based subjects, e.g. learners watch relevant videos and discuss different methods of achieving the same outcome, and then decide which is the most effective. This could be based on a real situation which has occurred that did not go well. Learners could discuss alternative ways to reach a better outcome.

Case studies encourage learners to undertake research, fact find, generate new ideas and make decisions. It can be used individually to support research and decision making, or when used with groups it can encourage teamwork and collaboration.

## Resources

- Access to a range of case studies – these might be provided for you or you may have to write your own

## Advantages

- Supports active learning
- Helps simplify complex subjects
- Assists learners in developing analytical skills
- Gives learners access to concepts which may otherwise be difficult to demonstrate, and which can support employability skills
- Can be inexpensive and time-saving

## Disadvantages

- It might take time for learners to master the activity
- Can be time-consuming to plan for, or to find appropriate materials
- There's a risk of not presenting all aspects of the subject

## How can I measure my learners' progress, meet individual needs and demonstrate stretch and challenge for all?

Observation of learner discussions in groups will support measuring individual contributions and progress. This can be concluded with each learner completing a task to identify their decision/choice and the reason behind it (written or verbal).

The case studies you provide can be differentiated to meet individual needs and to enable all learners to be stretched and challenged at the appropriate level for them. In addition, extension activities can be given to further build on the learning undertaken, e.g. learners could be asked to add further detail as to the reasons for their choice, or learners with opposing choices could be paired together to discuss and reach a compromise.

> **Tip**
>
> It can take learners a few attempts to fully engage in the case study so don't be perturbed if it doesn't work first time.

# Further reading and weblinks

Gravells A (2017) *Principles and Practices of Teaching and Training*: Learning Matters/Sage, London.

SimplyPsychology – *Case study method* – https://tinyurl.com/y2vquy3k

# 9 Catchphrase

| Individual | | Small group | √ | Large group | √ |
|---|---|---|---|---|---|
| Formative | √ | Summative | | Preparation time | 30 minutes plus |
| Informal | √ | Formal | | Timing | 40–60 minutes |
| British Values | * | Employability | * | After session marking? | |
| English | √ | Maths | * | Digital skills | |
| Entry Level | √ | Level 1 and 2 | √ | Level 3 upwards | √ |

*depends upon what and how you are planning to use the approach

## What is it?

Catchphrase is an activity to give learners the chance to guess what an image is, which is related to the current topic or subject.

A large image is displayed on a board relating to the current topic or subject, but is covered up in sections. The sections will be revealed as the activity progresses, e.g. for a group of learners who are studying electrics, the image could be a picture of a car racing track and a sheet of glass being smashed (to represent a circuit breaker). The image can be displayed electronically using a PowerPoint presentation, or it can be on a poster on the wall.

Learners are divided into two groups of between four and eight, and given a bell or a buzzer. To start the activity, a topic or subject-related question is asked and the group who buzzes or rings the bell first answers the question. If they answer correctly a section of the cover is removed revealing a piece of the image, and the group can have one guess as to what it is. If they guess correctly they have won the round, if they guess incorrectly the activity continues with another question.

If the group that buzzed or rang the bell answers the question incorrectly, the other group have a chance to answer. If they guess correctly, they can have a go at stating what the image is. The questions continue and every time a question is answered correctly, another piece of the image is uncovered, until one of the groups identifies what it is. The groups can confer prior to answering a question, but they run the risk of the other group pressing their buzzer or ringing their bell first.

You can plan to play one round with just one covered image or two or three rounds, but you will need a different topic or subject-related image for each round. You can decide how many pieces are used to reveal the image.

## What can it be used for?

Catchphrase is a fantastic activity which can be used at the start of the session to recap the previous session, or at the end of a session to amalgamate the learning which has taken place.

If your group is larger than 16 learners, you could have two or three learners taking turns to ask the questions, two or three learners keeping the scores, and one or two learners revealing the image. The groups can then be rotated after each round so that each group takes part in different aspects of the activity.

## Resources

- A bank of topic or subject-related images that can be covered in sections and displayed on a board (or created and used electronically)
- A bank of questions relating to the topic/subject
- A resource to record the scores (this can be electronic, a whiteboard or paper based)
- Buzzers or bells

## Advantages

👍 A fun and effective way of testing knowledge and understanding

👍 Supports active learning

👍 Visually stimulating

👍 Supports memory recall

## Disadvantages

👎 Not all learners may want to take part

👎 Requires learners to be self-motivated

👎 Not all learners will take it seriously

👎 Learners may become too competitive

## How can I measure my learners' progress, meet individual needs and demonstrate stretch and challenge for all?

Observing and listening to the learners conferring, and the answers to the questions will support you in identifying the progress they have made. The questions should vary from easy to hard to enable individuals to demonstrate stretch and challenge.

Depending on group needs and abilities, you could nominate a learner in each group to answer the question, and not allow conferring. This will help to ensure individual needs are met by matching the question to the learner's abilities.

To challenge learning further, you could use an image which relates to a relevant resource or technical word.

> ### Tip
>
> To make the game more fun, rather than giving the learners a buzzer or a bell, ask them to agree a sound they will make when they want to answer a question.

# Further reading and weblinks

ESLKidsGAMES – ESL Game: Catchphrase – http://tinyurl.com/y4huo77o

Trainerbubble – *Catchphrase game free training* – https://tinyurl.com/yyjylwu9

# 10 Charades

| Individual | | Small group | √ | Large group | √ |
|---|---|---|---|---|---|
| Formative | √ | Summative | | Preparation time | 30 minutes plus |
| Informal | √ | Formal | | Timing | 20–60 minutes |
| British Values | * | Employability | * | After session marking? | |
| English | √ | Maths | * | Digital skills | * |
| Entry Level | √ | Level 1 and 2 | √ | Level 3 upwards | √ |

*depends upon what and how you are planning to use the approach

## What is it?

Charades is an activity which requires a learner to mime without speaking, a word or phrase which is related to the current topic or subject. The rest of the group must try to guess what the word or phrase is.

Prior to the start of the session, you will need to prepare slips of paper or cards with topic or subject-related words or phrases on. You can then place these in a bowl or a box so the learners can't see them.

Divide the learners into two groups of equal size (nominate them as group A and group B). You will need to decide who goes into which group, and in what order the learners will participate. If you would rather not use A and B, you could use the names of colours or something else.

A learner from group A draws a slip out of the bowl or box and mimes the word or phrase to the rest of group A. Group A has three minutes to collaborate and guess the word or phrase. If they guess correctly within the three minutes, they gain a point; if they can't guess within the three minutes, group B (who have also been watching) can gain the point by guessing correctly.

The groups then swap over, draw out a new slip of paper and repeat, with a person from group B miming the word or phrase to their group (with group A watching).

Three or four rounds for each group will take about 60 minutes.

An alternative method is for the learner to describe (rather than mime) a subject-specific word or resource, without using key words, e.g. describing a *scarf* without using the word *neck*.

You will need to guide your learners regarding the gestures they can use, perhaps by having the following bullet points on display:

- Book title: Open and close your hands as if they were a book
- Movie title: Pretend to crank an old-fashioned movie camera
- Play title: Pretend to pull the rope that opens the theatre curtains
- Song title: Pretend to sing
- TV show: Draw a rectangle with your fingers
- Number of words in the title: Hold up the relevant number of fingers
- Which word you're working on: Hold up the number of fingers, e.g. two to denote the second word
- Number of syllables in the word: Lay the number of fingers on the inside of your arm, e.g. three fingers denotes three syllables
- Which syllable: Lay the relevant number of fingers on the outside of your arm
- Length of word: Make a *little* or *big* sign with your fingers or arms
- Sounds like: Cup one hand behind an ear

A whole group discussion should be held at the end of the activity to evaluate the learning which has taken place.

# What can it be used for?

Charades is a fun way to support learners to revise and recap. It can be used to start a session to check learning from a previous session, or at the end of a session as a summary.

# Resources

- A bank of words or phrases relating to the topic/subject written on slips of paper or cards
- A bowl or box to store the slips of paper
- A stopwatch or a timer
- A resource to record the points (this can be electronic, a whiteboard or paper based)

# Advantages

- A fun and effective way of testing knowledge and understanding
- Can be used at any point during the session
- Re-focuses groups
- Re-engages individuals

# Disadvantages

🖓 A shy or nervous learner may not engage well in this activity as they may struggle to answer in front of their peers (groups or teams could alleviate this)

🖓 Difficult to manage with a large group of learners

🖓 Learners may become too competitive

🖓 Time-consuming to set up (but can be used again with other learners)

# How can I measure my learners' progress, meet individual needs and demonstrate stretch and challenge for all?

Progress can be measured by observation of the learners miming the word or phrase and listening to who makes the correct guesses. Words and phrases can be differentiated using different coloured card or paper, from easy to hard. This will help to meet individual needs and to demonstrate stretch and challenge. Your knowledge of the learners could ensure they choose the right coloured card for a question at their level.

The whole group discussion at the end of the activity will support progress measures. You may need to ask directed questions to the quiet/shy learners to ensure they have developed their knowledge and understanding.

> ### Tip
> If you are working with a small group let them guess individually rather than collaborating with each other.

# Further reading and weblinks

Quizalize – *Top 10 classroom games* – https://tinyurl.com/yahqv9m8

Familyeducation – *How to play charades* – https://tinyurl.com/y8rkoygr

# 11 Concept mapping

| Individual | √ | Small group | √ | Large group | √ |
|---|---|---|---|---|---|
| Formative | √ | Summative | √ | Preparation time | 5–10 mins |
| Informal | √ | Formal | √ | Timing | 20–60 minutes |
| British Values | * | Employability | * | After session marking? | √ |
| English | √ | Maths | * | Digital skills | * |
| Entry Level | | Level 1 and 2 | * | Level 3 upwards | √ |

*depends upon what and how you are planning to use the approach*

## What is it?

Concept mapping is an activity to enable learners to create a type of graphic visual organiser. It will help them to organise and represent detailed knowledge regarding a subject. It can be carried out individually, in pairs or in groups.

It begins with the main idea (or concept) which the learners need to write or draw onto a blank piece of paper. Branches can then be drawn from the concept to show how the main idea can be broken down into specific subjects. It differs from a mind map (see Chapter 28) as it allows learners to focus on more than one idea or concept during the activity. Links to the original concept can be explored, as well as connections between the subjects which are added to the branches.

A mind map focuses on one concept and the branches remain in a radial structure. A concept map connects multiple concepts and ideas, and has many branches and clusters, a bit like a tree. When learners create a mind map, the process should be fast and spontaneous and reflect the learners' first thoughts regarding a subject.

When a learner creates a concept map, they should consider relationships between different concepts and ideas, representing them in words in a box or a circle, and then building on each of them, covering all actual cases or scenarios. Concept mapping should be factual, and learners should think in detail to cover all possible links.

Once learners have completed their concept maps, a short group discussion or paired activity should be held to check and correct any misconceptions.

## What can it be used for?

Concept mapping is an effective way for learners to develop visual processing, memory recall and concentration. It further develops the learners' logic and reasoning skills.

Concept mapping encourages learners to identify connections to a topic or a subject and enables them to focus on the essential facts by simple labelling in boxes, rather than reading or writing lots of text.

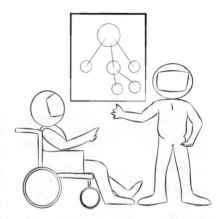

It's an ideal activity to use at the end of a module or unit as a summative assessment. Alternatively, it can be used at the start of a session as a recap from the previous session, where learners build a map that visually represents information that they remember.

## Resources

- Paper and pens (or electronic devices) for noting down findings and ideas

## Advantages

👍 Helps learners generate new ideas

👍 Encourages learners to discover new information by building on what they already know

👍 Supports learners to communicate ideas and thoughts

👍 Helps learners to enhance knowledge of any topic, and evaluate information

## Disadvantages

👎 Marking and assessment can be time-consuming

👎 Less visual or creative learners may struggle to engage with the activity

## How can I measure my learners' progress, meet individual needs and demonstrate stretch and challenge for all?

As learners create their concept maps, they are using perceptions and ideas they already know, making it an ideal tool to measure progress.

When marking and assessing the learners' concept map, you can identify what they do not understand. You can then target those individuals with developmental feedback, to help them evaluate and recognise what they need to do to improve. This helps meet their individual needs and demonstrates stretch and challenge.

## Tip

Encouraging learners to use coloured pens will aid creativity. Alternatively, concept maps could be created digitally, e.g. by using a computer or a suitable electronic device.

# Further reading and weblinks

BYU Centre For Teaching and Learning – *Concept mapping* – https://tinyurl.com/yaetqpul

Education Technology and Mobile Learning – *9 great concept mapping tools for teachers and students* – https://tinyurl.com/y7kvzn7h

# 12 Debates

| Individual | | Small group | √ | Large group | √ |
|---|---|---|---|---|---|
| Formative | √ | Summative | | Preparation time | 10–15 minutes |
| Informal | √ | Formal | | Timing | 20 minutes minimum |
| British Values | √ | Employability | √ | After session marking? | |
| English | √ | Maths | * | Digital skills | |
| Entry Level | | Level 1 and 2 | √ | Level 3 upwards | √ |

*depends upon what and how you are planning to use the approach

## What is it?

A debate is about learners deliberating and contemplating a topic which has opposing sides.

You will need to select a topic or subject which your learners can relate to, and which allows a two-sided discussion, one for and one against. It is usually best to group your learners so that no one learner has all the pressure to perform, and other learners can help with comprehension. Ideally, divide your learners into four teams with three to five learners in each team giving you two debating groups.

You could assign different topics to each of the debating groups to discuss, research and present. Alternatively, to save time, give two of the teams the positive aspects of the topics and the remaining teams the negative aspects of the topics.

Another way to facilitate this activity is to have a different team observe and act as judges, and vote which team presented the best case (i.e. positive or negative). The teams can then swap roles.

Timings should be given to the learners regarding how long they can have to develop a strategy for the debate, and how long each team has to present their case.

## What can it be used for?

Debates are a good way to summarise a topic or subject which learners have been working towards. It also helps learners to consider alternative points of view, supporting the development of employability skills and British Values.

Debates can also be used to introduce a new topic, e.g. a group of equine care learners could debate 'Should equine passports be optional?' or a group of computer learners could debate 'Does social media make us more alone?'.

## Resources required

- A list of questions based on relevant topics for the learners to debate

## Advantages

👍 Encourages research

👍 Develops speaking and listening skills

👍 Helps increase learner confidence and self-esteem in preparation for employment

👍 Allows freedom of viewpoints

👍 Demonstrates understanding

👍 Can be engaging and active for most learners

👍 Encourages learners to formulate an argument which is evidence based

👍 Encourages learners to embrace British Values

## Disadvantages

👎 Shy or less confident learners may not engage in the debate

👎 Can become personal to some learners, which could cause arguments outside of the learning environment

👎 Some learners might dominate, or become loud if the groups are not managed effectively throughout the activity

👎 Learners may need to research in advance of the activity

## How can I measure my learners' progress, meet individual needs and demonstrate stretch and challenge for all?

Progress measures will be made via observation of the debate and the outcome of the learners' vote. You may need to ask some specific questions of your own at the end of the activity to check each learner's knowledge and understanding

Differentiating the topic and careful grouping of learners will enable stretch and challenge and meet individual needs.

> **Tip**
>
> Make sure learners are clear regarding the time they have for each part of the activity.

# Further reading and weblinks

Educationworld – *Debates in the classroom* – https://tinyurl.com/y36m2t7c

TeachHub – *How to hold a classroom debate* – https://tinyurl.com/y2yu8rnm

# 13 Demonstration

| Individual | √ | Small group | √ | Large group | √ |
|---|---|---|---|---|---|
| Formative | √ | Summative | | Preparation time | 30 minutes plus |
| Informal | √ | Formal | | Timing | 10–40 minutes |
| British Values | * | Employability | √ | After session marking? | |
| English | * | Maths | * | Digital skills | * |
| Entry Level | √ | Level 1 and 2 | √ | Level 3 upwards | √ |

*depends upon what and how you are planning to use the approach*

## What is it?

A demonstration is an activity used by the teacher to show learners how to make or do something. It's given in a step-by-step approach to develop learners' technical skills. It can be a physical demonstration to teach a skill regarding how to practically do something, e.g. in first-aid you might demonstrate how to put a knee bandage onto a person, to enable learners to see how to do it. Or it can be a visual demonstration, e.g. using a flipchart or PowerPoint presentation to demonstrate visually how to do something.

During the demonstration, whether it be physical or visual, you should explain the main points and the significance of what you are doing, step by step. Keep explanations simple but ensure the necessary steps required to achieve the final outcome are covered.

It is useful to ask learners some questions throughout the process. This is to keep them engaged in what they are learning and to check they have understood what you are showing them. It is always good practice to leave a few minutes at the end of the demonstration to allow time for learners to ask you any questions.

## What can it be used for?

A demonstration can be used for just about anything you wish to communicate to learners to help them develop particular technical skills. It enables learners to see and then to imitate your actions, rather than having to learn through spoken words, reading text, or on their own. Asking learners some questions throughout the demonstration will keep them engaged and allow you to informally assess the learning which has taken place.

After the demonstration, learners could try out the activity on their own, in pairs, or small groups, depending upon how many resources you have.

## Resources

- Equipment and resources (if it's a practical demonstration)
- Notes of the step-by-step approach you will take
- Flipchart paper, posters or a projector if it's a visual demonstration
- A bank of questions to ask the learners as you progress through the demonstration

## Advantages

👍 Helps to improve understanding of a complex skill, as learners can see how to do something

👍 Can be motivational to learners as they can see an outcome or the end product

👍 Can speed up learning as learners can see how to apply the skills

👍 Can support the development of employability skills

## Disadvantages

👎 Can become disorganised if learners ask too many questions

👎 Generally, only suitable for technical skills

👎 Heavily reliant on resources

👎 Time-consuming to organise

## How can I measure my learners' progress, meet individual needs and demonstrate stretch and challenge for all?

It is important during the demonstration to ask learners differentiated questions to check knowledge and understanding, and to keep them engaged. Differentiated questions can be asked by skill, level or by complexity, e.g. in a media make-up session you may be demonstrating a particular *look*. A differentiated question for a higher skilled learner could be 'What other colour combinations could be used for this look?'. A lower skilled learner could be asked 'When could you use this look?'.

If you can let your learners repeat, practise and discuss what they have just seen, it will give them *hands-on* experience. This will allow you to observe what they have learned and supportively correct any misconceptions or mistakes to reinforce their learning.

The observation of learner skills will measure the progress they are making. You can also ask questions to individuals to stretch and challenge their knowledge and understanding regarding the subject.

Tip

Practise your demonstration beforehand to check your timings. Try not to read from your notes as you demonstrate, as this can put learners off watching you.

# Further reading and weblinks

Gravells A (2017) *Principles and Practices of Teaching and Training*: Learning Matters/Sage, London.

Petty G (2009) *Evidence-based Teaching: A Practical Approach* (2nd edn): Nelson Thornes, Cheltenham.

# 14 Discovery

| Individual | √ | Small group | √ | Large group | √ |
|---|---|---|---|---|---|
| Formative | √ | Summative | | Preparation time | 15 minutes |
| Informal | √ | Formal | | Timing | 30–60 minutes |
| British Values | * | Employability | √ | After session marking? | |
| English | * | Maths | * | Digital skills | * |
| Entry Level | √ | Level 1 and 2 | √ | Level 3 upwards | √ |

*depends upon what and how you are planning to use the approach

## What is it?

Discovery is about learners finding things out for themselves by doing something (if it's safe to do so) and by asking questions, e.g. discovering how to wire an electric plug. Working in pairs or small groups, learners can take a plug apart to see how it's put together (rather than just looking at diagrams). They can then put it back together for the teacher to check. Discovery also works for theoretical topics to promote problem-solving skills, research, questioning and discussion.

## What can it be used for?

Discovery is a fantastic activity which enables learners to interact with items, objects or equipment to find out how they work, or to solve a problem through trial and error, e.g. cookery learners could be tasked with creating and baking their own recipe for a meal. They would research the ingredients and then cook the meal, without referring to other recipes.

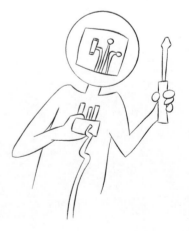

A discovery activity can be carried out individually or in groups, and the activities can be real or simulated. Learners can discover things for themselves, reflect on what they have achieved, and discuss their findings with their peers and you.

## Resources required

- Relevant items, objects or equipment
- Access to books and the internet for research (if applicable)

# Advantages

👍 Enables the learner to think about what they are doing

👍 Encourages engagement with the task

👍 Promotes curiosity, motivation and independence

👍 Develops creativity and problem-solving skills

👍 Encourages learners to ask 'why?'

# Disadvantages

👎 Enough resources are required for all learners

👎 Can be difficult to see what each learner is doing, if it's a practical activity

👎 Some learners might lack the confidence to work on their own

# How can I measure my learners' progress, meet individual needs and demonstrate stretch and challenge for all?

Observation of the practical tasks, along with questioning, will enable you to ascertain each learner's progress.

Some learners may already have a certain amount of skill and/or knowledge regarding a subject, whereas others won't. Knowing their starting points will help you gauge what activities you require them to do, e.g. a group of apprentice construction learners might consist of various levels of experience. Higher level learners could be challenged to build a wall of a certain height. Other learners could carry out smaller tasks such as mixing the mortar, before attempting to use a trowel, lay bricks and use a spirit level. As you observe their progress, you can stretch the learners with further tasks.

> **Tip**
>
> If you have a large group, encourage experienced learners to work with inexperienced learners so that they can learn from and support each other.

# Further reading and weblinks

Principles of Learning – *Discovery Learning* (Jerome Bruner) – https://tinyurl.com/y2dmhjua

TeAchnology – *What is discovery learning?* – https://tinyurl.com/y3gbcoql

# 15 Field trip

| Individual | √ | Small group | √ | Large group | √ |
|---|---|---|---|---|---|
| Formative | √ | Summative | | Preparation time | 30 minutes plus |
| Informal | √ | Formal | | Timing | Full session |
| British Values | * | Employability | √ | After session marking? | * |
| English | * | Maths | * | Digital skills | * |
| Entry Level | √ | Level 1 and 2 | √ | Level 3 upwards | √ |

*depends upon what and how you are planning to use the approach

## What is it?

A field trip is about visiting a relevant venue or environment to support learning which is related to the current topic or subject, e.g. agricultural learners could visit an agricultural show to watch demonstrations and speak to exhibitors about new technologies. This is an area which they would otherwise not be able to access.

Learners could be involved in the planning process to give them ownership of the trip. This might include fact finding or planning the itinerary for the day. In addition, learners should be involved in setting a few ground rules regarding attitude and behaviour, as they are representing their organisation as ambassadors.

Learners should be given a *brief* prior to the trip instructing them what they must do or find out during their visit.

It is important to follow your own organisation's policies and procedures. Field trips must be planned in advance to ensure adequate insurance, safeguarding and risk assessments are in place. Written parental permission might be needed prior to the trip. Transport and any financial costs also need to be agreed and paid in advance of the trip. It is advisable to take a first-aider with you and to have an emergency contact number for each of your learners, just in case of an incident. If any learners have any particular requirements, e.g. access or dietary, these will need to be taken into account.

## What can it be used for?

Field trips are an excellent way to put theory into practice, to develop employability skills and to bring learning to life, as learners will be seeing something first-hand in a real environment. The term *field* doesn't mean it takes place in a field, it can be anywhere, e.g. a museum, a factory, the theatre or an historical site.

It is important that learners are briefed and fully understand what they are supposed to do or find out during the field trip, otherwise it will become a day out with little learning taking place. In addition, you should plan to de-brief the learners after the field trip has taken place. This de-briefing could lead to further learning activities, e.g. a case study or question-and-answer session.

## Resources

- Transport (to and from the venue)
- Tickets into the venue (if required)
- Adequate staff supervision for the number of learners
- Paper and pens (or electronic devices) for noting down findings and ideas

## Advantages

👍 Brings learning to life

👍 Connects learners to the real world

👍 Helps put theory into practice

👍 Can develop employability skills (depending on the nature of the field trip)

## Disadvantages

👎 Needs careful planning and budgeting

👎 Health and safety, and other organisational policies and procedures must be followed

👎 Supervision is usually required at all times

## How can I measure my learners' progress, meet individual needs and demonstrate stretch and challenge for all?

The brief given out to your learners regarding what they must do during the visit could be differentiated to meet individual needs, and to stretch and challenge all learners, e.g. learners at an agricultural show must identify six different breeds of sheep and four different breeds of cattle. To differentiate this: all learners must identify a use for one of the breeds; most learners must identify a use for two of the breeds; and some learners must identify a use for all of the breeds.

Further stretch and challenge could be to ask the learners to act as judges and to place the breeds in what they think will be the winning order. They can then be asked to compare their decisions with the judges' decisions and identify why the judge placed each animal in that particular order.

Carefully planned learning activities after the field trip, e.g. a case study (see Chapter 8) will support you to measure the impact of the field trip upon learning, and the individual progress made.

---

### Tip

When devising your scheme of work, plan the date for the field trip around a relevant topic or subject being taught at that time. This will ensure you have plenty of time to plan and organise the event, to carry out any necessary risk assessments, and to stay within budget.

---

## Further reading and weblinks

Gravells A (2017) *Principles and Practices of Teaching and Training*: Learning Matters/Sage, London.

Teach Thought – *The benefits of learning through field trips* – https://tinyurl.com/yc4dvrg4

# 16 Find your match

| Individual | | Small group | √ | Large group | √ |
|---|---|---|---|---|---|
| Formative | √ | Summative | | Preparation time | 30 minutes plus |
| Informal | √ | Formal | | Timing | 20–30 minutes |
| British Values | * | Employability | * | After session marking? | |
| English | √ | Maths | * | Digital skills | |
| Entry Level | √ | Level 1 and 2 | √ | Level 3 upwards | |

*depends upon what and how you are planning to use the approach*

## What is it?

Find your match is an activity which gets your learners up and moving around the learning environment in anticipation of matching a related card with another learner's card.

You will need to prepare the cards prior to the start of the session. The cards should be small enough for the learners to hold but large enough for them to be able to see and read clearly. They should be made as pairs and link to the current topic or subject, e.g. for a group studying English, the cards could be words which have synonyms or antonyms. Or for a group studying maths, one card could have a sum and the other card the correct answer.

The activity can also be used for vocational subjects, e.g. a group studying sports could have a card with an image of goalposts and the matching card is the image of a goalkeeper.

Learners should be handed one card each, and must find their match by asking questions of their peers. When answering questions about the matching card, learners can only answer *yes* or *no*. When asking the questions, learners cannot directly ask about the answer, e.g. the learner looking for a match for the goalpost can't ask 'Are you a goalkeeper?', but they can ask 'Do you play football?'. At no point must a learner show their card to another learner, even if they believe they have found their match.

When the learners believe they have found their match, both learners should go to the teacher and explain why they believe they are a match. If they are correct, they can sit down. If they are incorrect, they must continue with the activity until they find their match.

## What can it be used for?

Find your match is a good activity to use to revise and recap prior learning, and to check knowledge and understanding of related themes. It can be used to start a session to check learning from a previous session, or at the end of a session as a summary.

It's also a great way to encourage your learners to interact with each other and develop their social and communication skills.

## Resources

• Pre-prepared cards with the desired topic or subject-related information on

## Advantages

👍 A fun and effective way of testing knowledge and understanding

👍 Can be used at any point during the session

👍 Re-focuses groups

👍 Re-engages individuals

👍 Helps to develop communication skills

👍 Can be differentiated to meet individual needs

## Disadvantages

👎 Time-consuming to prepare and carry out

👎 The learners can soon get very loud if not fully managed

👎 Assumes learners are confident to engage in a discussion using questions

👎 Can be dominated by the more confident learners

# How can I measure my learners' progress, meet individual needs and demonstrate stretch and challenge for all?

To measure progress, observe the activity and listen to the questions learners are asking each other. In addition, when the learners believe they have found their match, there is an opportunity to ask direct questions to stretch and challenge individuals, even if they have not found the correct match.

The cards can be differentiated to meet individual needs, e.g. for learners of a low ability, simple images can be used to pair up; for those of a high ability, complex words or numbers can be used. To help you know which is which, you could use different coloured card.

Differentiation could also be met by giving a specific card to each learner, rather than issuing these randomly.

> **Tip**
>
> If you laminate the cards they can be used again with future groups.

# Further reading and weblinks

Gravells A (2017) *Principles and Practices of Teaching and Training*: Learning Matters/Sage, London.

Icebreakers.ws – *Who's my match* – https://tinyurl.com/y3ffb3v3

# 17 Flipped classroom

| Individual | √ | Small group | √ | Large group | √ |
|---|---|---|---|---|---|
| Formative | √ | Summative | | Preparation time | 30 minutes plus |
| Informal | √ | Formal | | Timing | 30 minutes plus |
| British Values | * | Employability | √ | After session marking? | * |
| English | * | Maths | * | Digital skills | √ |
| Entry Level | | Level 1 and 2 | √ | Level 3 upwards | √ |

*depends upon what and how you are planning to use the approach

## What is it?

The flipped classroom (also known as flipped learning) is a blended learning approach which reverses, or *flips*, the traditional learning environment. It mixes face-to-face interaction during a session with independent study and research outside of the session.

Learners can watch a pre-recorded session or online video, listen to podcasts (which can be instructional and/or interactive) or carry out research at home or elsewhere. They then attend the class session to practise their skills and deepen their knowledge and understanding. The class session therefore becomes a forum for the exploration of topics in greater detail.

## What can it be used for?

It can be used to introduce learners to a particular topic, subject or course material prior to the class session, to enable them to explore it further during the session.

It's an excellent way to introduce a new topic or encourage advanced concepts, problem solving, independent thinking and learning skills.

It can also be used for revision and recapping a previous topic, or to strengthen or expand on a subject previously taught.

It's an ideal activity for apprentices to use as part of their off-the-job training. The research could be linked to different brands or companies to further develop employer engagement and employability skills.

It can encourage learners to carry out activities away from the classroom, e.g. in a library, museum or working environment. This would help promote independent working and employability skills.

# Resources

- A relevant device or equipment to create a video or podcast
- A pre-prepared list of relevant online videos if you are not creating your own
- A learning platform such as Moodle for all learners to access the materials which you need to upload (if applicable)

# Advantages

👍 Learners have control of what they learn and when (learning at their own pace providing it's completed prior to the required session)

👍 It promotes learner-centered learning and problem solving

👍 It can be more efficient for the organisation and learners (courses can be delivered in a shorter time frame)

👍 If recorded electronically, videos can be viewed several times to aid understanding, and reduce the pressure on the learner of having to remember everything at once

👍 Enables discussions to take place during the session based on what has been learnt outside of the session

# Disadvantages

👎 Planning and implementation can be time-consuming to begin with (but once prepared it can be used again)

👎 Requires learners to be self-motivated and have some basic computing skills

👎 Learners will need a suitable device and internet access if required

👎 Not all learners will engage with the concept and some may fall behind

👎 Increases screen time for learners who may already have high screen use

# How can I measure my learners' progress, meet individual needs and demonstrate stretch and challenge for all?

You should ask your learners to devise their own questions about the topic, and bring them to the face-to-face session for discussion. You can have a bank of pre-prepared questions ready to test and probe your learners' knowledge and understanding further.

Learners can work in small groups to present the information to their peers (and to you) using *watch, summarise* and *question* (see Chapter 47), which is a great way to address any misconceptions.

You can ask your learners to complete an evaluation of their own learning, e.g. how they approached the activity, what they learnt, and what they would like to explore further.

If you are making a visual recording, it should be short and to the point to gain learner attention. You will need to consider different learning approaches to meet individual needs, and whether there are enough activities to engage everyone.

As learners have already been introduced to the session beforehand, you will have time during the session to work with individuals. This would benefit those who would not usually engage in direct question-and-answer sessions.

## Tip

If you are creating a video, it's important to practise in front of the camera before recording and sharing it with your learners. You will need to focus on your timings, voice tone, background and lighting, e.g. are there too many pauses, are the images clear and well lit, what is the sound quality like, what will the learners be looking at, and what do you want them to do now?

# Further reading and weblinks

AdvancedHE – *Flipped learning* – https://tinyurl.com/ydddeudn

Bergmann J and Sams A (2012) *Flip Your Classroom:* International Society for Technology in Education, Washington.

Teachthought – *The definition of the flipped classroom* – https://tinyurl.com/yccqplrw

# 18 Guess who or what

| Individual | | Small group | √ | Large group | √ |
|---|---|---|---|---|---|
| Formative | √ | Summative | | Preparation time | 10 minutes |
| Informal | √ | Formal | | Timing | 20–45 minutes |
| British Values | * | Employability | * | After session marking? | |
| English | * | Maths | * | Digital skills | * |
| Entry Level | √ | Level 1 and 2 | √ | Level 3 upwards | |

*depends upon what and how you are planning to use the approach

## What is it?

Guess who or what is an activity where learners are allocated a current topic or subject-related picture or technical word, without knowing who or what it is. They then have to make a guess.

The topic or subject-related picture or technical word is attached to the clothes at the back of each learner without them seeing what it is. They must move around the learning environment and ask their peers some questions until they make a correct guess. The aim of the activity is for the learner to guess the answer in the shortest time. Once this has been achieved, and depending upon time, the other learners could continue.

Prior to the session, you will need to select topic or subject-related pictures or photographs (these can be whole or cut in half depending on how difficult you want to make the activity). Alternatively, you can write a technical word or a person's name (related to the subject, e.g. a famous person) on paper. You can either use double-sided sticky tape, sticky notes or something similar for each picture or word, to enable them to be temporarily attached.

An alternative method to this activity is to place the learners into pairs, give them some sticky notes and let them devise and write a technical word for each other. They then stick it on each other's forehead and take turns in asking questions until they guess who or what it is which is on their own forehead.

## What can it be used for?

This is an excellent activity to use to rejuvenate learners. It can be fun and lively and requires the learners to move around the learning space rather than be sat still.

It is a good tool to test individuals' knowledge and understanding prior to summative assessment as it requires learners to revisit prior learning.

## Resources

- Pre-prepared sticky notes or pictures with the desired topic or subject-related information
- Safety pins if attaching the paper to the backs of learners' clothes

## Advantages

👍 A fun and effective way of testing knowledge and understanding

👍 Can be used at any point during the session

👍 Re-focuses groups

👍 Rejuvenates individuals

👍 Can be differentiated to meet individual needs

👍 It's engaging and supports social learning

👍 Can make learning fun

## Disadvantages

👎 Difficult to manage with a large group of learners

👎 Learners may become too competitive and disruptive

👎 Can seem trivial to some learners

👎 Time-consuming to prepare and carry out (but can be used again with other learners)

# How can I measure my learners' progress, meet individual needs and demonstrate stretch and challenge for all?

By observing and listening to the questions the learners are asking to get clues, and by the way the question is answered, enables you to make progress measures regarding their knowledge and understanding.

The task can be differentiated by giving simpler pictures or words to the learners who are working at a lower level. Learners working at higher levels can be stretched and challenged by giving them a more technical picture or word.

If you are using the alternative version of this activity, pair your learners with someone who is working at the same level, and only allow them to answer *yes* or *no* to the questions to make the activity more challenging.

> **Tip**
>
> If you laminate the topic or subject-related pictures or technical words and use double-sided sticky tape, the tape can be removed at the end of the activity. The pictures and technical words can then be used again with future learners.

## Further reading and weblinks

HobbyLark – *How to play the guessing game "Who am I"* – http://tinyurl.com/y3pyogcx

Study.com – *What is interactive learning? Overview and tools* – http://tinyurl.com/y5r5jasj

# 19 Guest speakers

| Individual | √ | Small group | √ | Large group | √ |
|---|---|---|---|---|---|
| Formative | √ | Summative | | Preparation time | 30 minutes plus |
| Informal | √ | Formal | √ | Timing | * |
| British Values | * | Employability | √ | After session marking? | * |
| English | * | Maths | * | Digital skills | * |
| Entry Level | √ | Level 1 and 2 | √ | Level 3 upwards | √ |

*depends upon what and how you are planning to use the approach

## What is it?

A guest speaker is a subject expert who you can invite to share their skills, knowledge and understanding with your learners. They will enhance your session by giving real-life experience from the perspective of someone who has, or is, currently working in the subject or industry area.

## What can it be used for?

Guest speakers are the ideal people to support demonstrations, lectures, presentations or question-and-answer sessions. Ideally, they will currently be working in industry and an expert in the subject. They can help support your learners in developing their skills, knowledge and understanding, which will help prepare them for the world of work or higher levels of learning.

## Resources

• A subject expert guest speaker

## Advantages

👍 Enables a different focus regarding the subject

👍 Reinforces the subject and links it to employment

👍 Adds variety and expertise

👍 Learners can devise appropriate questions in advance and interact with the speaker

# Disadvantages

- It can be time-consuming to research who the subject experts are, to make contact with them, and to plan for their visit
- Needs to be planned well in advance as some speakers are very busy
- Some guest speakers may charge a fee and/or expenses
- Learners may not find the speaker very engaging
- The guest speaker must be supervised at all times and you must monitor all discussions (you will need to follow safeguarding and Prevent Duty procedures)

# How can I measure my learners' progress, meet individual needs and demonstrate stretch and challenge for all?

You could ask questions (or ask the speaker to ask questions) to enable stretch and challenge, and to support those who may not have understood something.

If you have a large group, you could summarise what the speaker has said, or ask the learners to write a short summary. You could read these after the session to gauge what has been learnt.

Higher level learners could write a reflective account to identify what they have learnt, which you can then read.

You could ask your learners (in small groups) to write down what they have learnt, and they could then present this to the rest of the learners (either at the end of the session or the beginning of the next session) with you observing.

---

### Tip

Photos regarding the visit by the guest speaker (with relevant permissions) could be taken and used to promote your organisation and theirs. Learners could collaborate to write a letter of thanks to the guest speaker and outline how they have benefitted from their visit. This might even lead to the learners being invited to the guest speaker's place of work to see theory in practice.

---

# Further reading and weblinks

Gross Davis B (2009) *Tools for Teaching* (2nd edn): Jossey-Bass, San Francisco.

Teach Hub – Classroom Management: *Guest speakers supporting learning* – https://tinyurl.com/y9hlz5un

Teaching on Purpose – *Guest Speakers: A Great Way to Commit to Education* – https://tinyurl.com/y7aof2hg

# 20   Half and half

| Individual | | Small group | √ | Large group | √ |
|---|---|---|---|---|---|
| Formative | √ | Summative | | Preparation time | 30 minutes plus |
| Informal | √ | Formal | | Timing | 45–60 minutes |
| British Values | * | Employability | * | After session marking? | * |
| English | √ | Maths | * | Digital skills | * |
| Entry Level | | Level 1 and 2 | * | Level 3 upwards | √ |

*depends upon what and how you are planning to use the approach

## What is it?

Half and half is about dividing your group into two halves and using two different approaches to learning.

One half of the group are given 20 minutes to research a topic or subject. The research material can be provided or the learners can carry out independent research. The other half attend a 20-minute lecture with the teacher, regarding the same topic or subject. The learners then swap activities and repeat for 20 minutes.

When everyone has completed the research activity and attended the lecture, they must pair up with a peer from the opposite group and for ten minutes discuss the key points they have learned, noting down any areas that differ.

Ideally the learners who are undertaking the research activity will have access to a separate room or a library to work independently.

The final part of half and half is a whole group discussion which could include directed questions to check learners' knowledge and understanding.

## What can it be used for?

Half and half is a great way to encourage learners to take responsibility for their own learning. It introduces research techniques which are supported by the lecture. In addition, the paired activity and whole group discussion at the end can correct any misconceptions and emphasise key learning points.

## Resources

- Access to research material, e.g. the internet, books and journals
- Lecture notes and/or materials

## Advantages

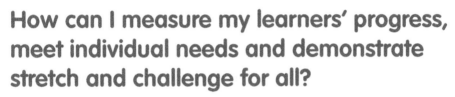

👍 Helps to develop research skills

👍 Supports reasoning and critical thinking skills

👍 Can improve learner confidence

👍 Encourages communication

## Disadvantages

👎 Not all learners will engage with the activity

👎 If both groups are in the same room for the lecture and the research, it could be noisy

# How can I measure my learners' progress, meet individual needs and demonstrate stretch and challenge for all?

The different sections of the activity – research, lecture, paired work and discussion – cover a range of learning preferences, helping to meet individual needs. It may be necessary to give clear written instructions for the research activity, to ensure learners fully engage in the time given.

The research activity could be differentiated by ability or level, and by planning who works with whom during the paired discussion. During the whole group discussion at the end of the activity, concepts may change again, challenging learners' thought processes.

To help measure individual progress, ensure you move around the learning environment during the paired discussion, after both activities have taken place, listening and observing these.

The whole group discussion at the end of the activity will support you to identify individual progress. You could also ask learners to write down one or two key points they have learned.

To further stretch and challenge individuals, you could ask differentiated directed questions.

---

### Tip

Prior to using this activity, consider how you will split your group into two halves, and who to pair with whom for the discussion. Advance planning will ensure good group dynamics and peer working.

---

## Further reading and weblinks

Forsyth Donelson R (2017) *Group Dynamics*: Cengage Learning Ltd, Boston.

Prodigy – *15 easy peer teaching strategies to help students* – https://tinyurl.com/ycocb6dj

# 21 Hot potato

| Individual | | Small group | √ | Large group | √ |
|---|---|---|---|---|---|
| Formative | √ | Summative | | Preparation time | 10 minutes |
| Informal | √ | Formal | | Timing | 15–20 minutes |
| British Values | √ | Employability | √ | After session marking? | * |
| English | √ | Maths | * | Digital skills | |
| Entry Level | | Level 1 and 2 | √ | Level 3 upwards | √ |

*depends upon what and how you are planning to use the approach

## What is it?

Hot potato is a way of building upon the knowledge and understanding from within a group.

Learners are placed into smaller groups of four to six. Each learner in the group is given a sheet of paper with a different topic or question written at the top of the page. Learners are given two minutes to write down as many key points as they can which relate to the topic or question on the sheet of paper.

When the time is up, the paper is then passed on to the person on their left who must read what is already written, and add their own responses in the time allocated, on the same sheet of paper.

Learners must not repeat other learners' responses. The sheet of paper keeps getting passed around the group until it is back with the original learner. For example, learners are placed into groups of four and are each given a piece of paper with one of the following British Values' headings on:

1. Democracy
2. The rule of law
3. Individual liberty
4. Mutual respect for tolerance of those with different faiths and beliefs and for those without faith.

Each learner must write down key words on their piece of paper, then pass it on to the next learner.

The paper is passed around the group to give all learners the chance to add their key words, without repeating any previous words.

The group then share their papers and hold a five-minute discussion identifying any statements or answers they had not thought of, or any which they think are not right.

If there is time, you could compare and contrast the whole group's papers and have a further discussion.

# What can it be used for?

Hot potato is an ideal activity to use part way through a topic or subject to amalgamate the learning undertaken so far. It is also an ideal recap activity as it encourages the learners to revisit prior learning.

You should emphasise how learners should respect and embrace each other's opinions, and how communication will support them in developing their knowledge and understanding of British Values, further developing their employability skills.

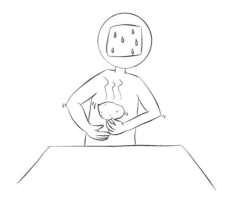

# Resources

- Sheets of paper with different topics or questions written at the top – one for each learner
- Pens

# Advantages

- Encourages independent thinking skills
- A fun and effective way of testing knowledge and understanding
- Can be used at any point during the session
- Re-engages individuals
- Good for quiet or shy learners as they can write down their answers without having to speak in front of others

# Disadvantages

- Not all learners may want to take part, and some might need support
- Requires learners to be self-motivated
- Not all learners will take it seriously

# How can I measure my learners' progress, meet individual needs and demonstrate stretch and challenge for all?

Observing what the learners are writing will enable you to see individual learners demonstrate their current knowledge and understanding. The group discussion at the end of the activity will also support you in identifying progress.

Knowing the learners' starting points and grouping the learners is key to meeting individual needs, e.g. learners of the same ability or level should be in the same group to enable you to give them topics or questions at the right level. This will also ensure learners are stretched and challenged to their full potential.

---

### Tip

A graffiti wall is a variation of the hot potato activity and useful for large groups. Topics or questions are written on flipchart paper and placed around the room. Learners work in teams of four to six learners to answer, with one member of the team scribing, before moving on to the next sheet and repeating.

---

# Further reading and weblinks

ESOL online – *Hot potato* – https://tinyurl.com/y62btce7

Laura Odgers – *Hot potato* – https://tinyurl.com/y3exjz2p

# 22 Inner and outer circles

| Individual | | Small group | √ | Large group | √ |
|---|---|---|---|---|---|
| Formative | √ | Summative | | Preparation time | 10 minutes |
| Informal | √ | Formal | | Timing | 30–60 minutes |
| British Values | * | Employability | * | After session marking? | |
| English | √ | Maths | * | Digital skills | |
| Entry Level | | Level 1 and 2 | √ | Level 3 upwards | √ |

*depends upon what and how you are planning to use the approach

## What is it?

Inner and outer circles is a problem solving, debating and/or discussion activity. It is sometimes referred to as *fish bowl*.

Six to eight learners sit or stand in a circle in the centre of the room (the inner circle). They are given an activity and must discuss it or act it out. The activity should relate to a relevant topic or subject which draws on the skills, knowledge and understanding of everyone in the group. The rest of the learners sit or stand in a larger circle (the outer circle), and observe and make notes regarding what happens. Those in the outer circle can then question and/or give feedback to those in the inner circle. The groups then swap places and repeat.

## What can it be used for?

This is a fantastic activity to encourage independent learning, problem-solving skills, and building relationships and trust between learners. Group sizes can vary from between two to eight learners in the inner circle and a larger group of learners in the outer circle, depending on your group and room size.

## Resources

- An area large enough for seating the two circles
- A pre-prepared activity such as a question, task or assignment
- Paper and pens (or electronic devices) for noting down findings and ideas

## Advantages

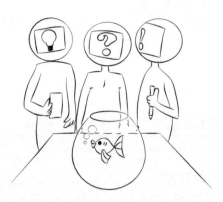

- 👍 Can be used for most group sizes (i.e. six learners upwards)
- 👍 Easy to differentiate the activity to suit the needs of the learners
- 👍 Very good way of developing trust and teamwork between learners
- 👍 Timings of the activity can be varied to suit the needs of the learners
- 👍 Excellent way to develop problem-solving, listening and communication skills

## Disadvantages

- 👎 Learners may get a little overexcited
- 👎 Some learners might dominate the activity
- 👎 Shy learners might not want to participate
- 👎 Teacher must facilitate the activity to enable everyone to take part
- 👎 It may be necessary to move the furniture in the room
- 👎 Can be time-consuming to carry out

## How can I measure my learners' progress, meet individual needs and demonstrate stretch and challenge for all?

You will be able to observe how your learners demonstrate their skills, knowledge, and/or understanding. Further questions can be asked by you (or the learners) to enable them to demonstrate deeper understanding.

The groups for the inner circle learners should be pre-planned to enable you to set appropriate activities which stretch and challenge each individual. The activity should relate to the current topic or subject to enable learners to demonstrate the progress they have made from their starting points.

Appropriate tasks should be set to meet the needs of the learners, i.e. at different levels of difficulty.

Additional tasks can be set for the outer circle, e.g. each learner could ask one relevant question of an inner circle learner. Alternatively, selected learners (chosen by you or by an inner circle learner) could ask further questions and/or give feedback to those in the inner circle, depending on the desired outcome and the time available.

> **Tip**
>
> If your learners are not confident to receive feedback in front of their peers, you could ask them to work in pairs to discuss and evaluate what they have learnt.

# Further reading and weblinks

kstoolkit – *Fish Bowl* – https://tinyurl.com/ybdx5j98

readwritethink – *Conducting inner-outer circle discussions* https://tinyurl.com/ycplcajc

# 23   Interleaving

| Individual | √ | Small group | √ | Large group | √ |
|---|---|---|---|---|---|
| Formative | √ | Summative | | Preparation time | * |
| Informal | √ | Formal | | Timing | * |
| British Values | * | Employability | * | After session marking? | |
| English | * | Maths | * | Digital skills | * |
| Entry Level | | Level 1 and 2 | √ | Level 3 upwards | √ |

*depends upon what and how you are planning to use the approach*

## What is it?

Interleaving is about mixing different topics or subjects, usually two or three, in the same session, rather than focusing on a single topic or subject.

Interleaving is delivered in the following format of a,b,c,a,b,c topics, whereas a traditional delivery would be in aaa, bbb, ccc topics, e.g. a learner could dedicate some time to maths, some time to biology, and some time to chemistry. Another example is learning to play the guitar. Rather than asking a learner to master one skill at a time such as reading music, learning chords or fingerstyle, they would spend an equal amount of time on each discipline during their study session.

Prior to starting an interleaving session, you will need to fully brief your learners and ask them to consider the amount of time they would like to spend on a topic or subject before changing it. Each learner should then discuss it with a peer (see Chapter 41: Think, pair and share) followed by agreement with the whole group, e.g. a three-hour study session could be broken into three one-hour sessions. Alternatively, learners may wish to spend more time on a particular theme and divide the three-hour session into one two-hour and two half-hour slots.

Ideally the topics or subjects should be related to enhance the learning experience.

## What can it be used for?

Interleaving is an effective activity for increasing learners' motor skills, e.g. in sports or practical sessions, learners are developing a range of skills which are required to master the topics or subjects. It is also a great extension or homework activity as learners spend short bursts of time studying the first topic or subject, and then move on to the second for the same (or similar) amount of time, before moving on to the third.

## Resources

- Depends on the topics or subjects being taught

## Advantages

- 👍 Supports critical thinking skills
- 👍 Strengthens memory and recall
- 👍 Does not require any additional resources or time

## Disadvantages

- 👎 Can be complicated to use at first
- 👎 Requires careful planning
- 👎 Learners must be able to concentrate and focus for set times

## How can I measure my learners' progress, meet individual needs and demonstrate stretch and challenge for all?

Learner progress should be continually monitored by observation during the session, and marking and assessment of their work.

Tasks should be set at the appropriate level to meet individual needs. An initial assessment should be carried out before attempting interleaving to enable stretch and challenge to be demonstrated.

> ### Tip
>
> Beware of learners switching topics or subjects if they find the current theme too challenging. Encourage learners to end each theme on a positive learning experience before moving on.

## Further reading and weblinks

Academic Affairs – https://tinyurl.com/ycrjgamn

Scientific American – https://tinyurl.com/ybqmrtxs

# 24 Jigsaw puzzle

| Individual | | Small group | √ | Large group | √ |
|---|---|---|---|---|---|
| Formative | √ | Summative | | Preparation time | 30 minutes plus |
| Informal | √ | Formal | | Timing | 15–30 minutes |
| British Values | * | Employability | * | After session marking? | |
| English | * | Maths | * | Digital skills | * |
| Entry Level | √ | Level 1 and 2 | √ | Level 3 upwards | √ |

*depends upon what and how you are planning to use the approach

## What is it?

Jigsaw puzzle is a group activity where learners have between 15 to 30 minutes to assemble a picture which is related to the current topic or subject, e.g. if you have 30 learners you could have five pictures with six pieces (one piece per learner). Mix the pieces up and give one to each learner. They will need to communicate with the others to find out who has the missing pieces to complete the jigsaw.

You could have a copy of the completed pictures on separate tables for the learners to locate first (by comparing their piece to it). Alternatively, you could try not showing a complete picture if you would like to challenge your learners further. However, this may take much longer for them to achieve.

At the end of the activity a five-minute group discussion should take place to confirm learning.

An alternative version of this activity would be for the learners to create the jigsaw puzzles as well as a suitable question which is related to each part of it.

## What can it be used for?

Jigsaw puzzle is a great way to develop learners' communication and teambuilding skills which helps to extend their employability skills. It also helps to develop learners' visual-processing and concentration skills. It can be used at the start of a session to recap previous learning or part way through a session to measure progress.

## Resources

- Jigsaw puzzles
- A suitable area to assemble the puzzles
- Some pre-prepared questions regarding the picture

# Advantages

👍 It's engaging and supports social learning

👍 Helps to develop employability and communication skills

👍 Can make learning fun

👍 Great for learners who are usually unwilling to participate in group work

# Disadvantages

👎 Less visual or creative learners may struggle to engage with the activity

👎 Not all learners will take the activity seriously

# How can I measure my learners' progress, meet individual needs and demonstrate stretch and challenge for all?

Observing the learners communicating and undertaking the activity will support you in measuring individual progress.

You can differentiate the activity by using different pictures at varying levels to meet individual needs.

Some groups will finish more quickly than others, so you can therefore set them a task based on the picture to stretch and challenge them, e.g. if the group are studying travel and tourism, the jigsaw could be a map of a country. The more able learners can then state things about that country such as its currency, major tourist attractions, transport links, the language spoken, and the colours of the national flag.

> ### Tip
>
> To save costs you can make the jigsaw yourself. Find a few pictures from old magazines or newspapers which relate to the topic or subject. You can then cut them into smaller shapes. You could also laminate them to use again with different learners.

# Further reading and weblinks

Gravells A (2017) *Principles and Practices of Teaching and Training*: Learning Matters/Sage, London.

Study.com – *What is interactive learning? Overview and tools* – http://tinyurl.com/y5r5jasj

# 25  Labelling

| Individual | √ | Small group | √ | Large group | √ |
|---|---|---|---|---|---|
| Formative | √ | Summative | √ | Preparation time | 15–30 minutes |
| Informal | √ | Formal | √ | Timing | 20–50 minutes |
| British Values | * | Employability | * | After session marking? | |
| English | * | Maths | * | Digital skills | * |
| Entry Level | √ | Level 1 and 2 | √ | Level 3 upwards | √ |

*depends upon what and how you are planning to use the approach

## What is it?

Labelling is about learners identifying the component parts of something and placing a label on it.

Learners are given a picture or a resource related to the current topic or subject: this could be live, e.g. a human being or an animal, or something inanimate, e.g. an engine or a scale model. The learners are asked to label the components or parts of it.

Learners can be given prepopulated labels or paper to create their own labels and stick onto the relevant component or part of the resource. Learners will individually place the labels where they think they should be. They can swap it with a peer's and look at each other's work, identifying and discussing any differences in the placing of the labels.

Learners can then choose to move their labels to match those of their peers or leave them as they are. Once they have completed the discussion with their peers you can check the placing of the labels is correct and challenge any mistakes.

## What can it be used for?

Labelling can be used at the beginning of a topic or subject as an initial assessment or at the end of a session to measure progress. It is a great activity for developing memory and recall, particularly for learners who need to remember components and parts of a piece of equipment, machinery or object. For example, learners who are taking a level three land-based engineering programme are required to service and repair engines and components. To do this they first need to be able to recognise and recall the parts of the engine. The learners could work individually, in pairs or small groups in a workshop and label the engine. Another example is that a learner studying human anatomy could label the largest and strongest muscles on one of their peers, and then swap over.

## Resources

- A topic or subject-related piece of equipment, machinery, picture or object
- Labels (prepopulated or blank)

## Advantages

- Aids memory recall
- Can be fun and engaging
- Encourages collaboration
- Visual and physical activity to keep learners active

## Disadvantages

- Can be time-consuming
- Not always possible to access a relevant piece of equipment, machinery or object
- Not all learners may want or be able to participate

# How can I measure my learners' progress, meet individual needs and demonstrate stretch and challenge for all?

Progress measures include observing the learners individually labelling their resource, listening to the peer discussion, and checking the learners' work at the end of the discussion.

The task can be differentiated to ensure every learner is stretched and challenged to their full potential by the resource, e.g. some learners could label the tractor engine, whilst others label the transmission gears. Or some learners could label the major muscles in the human body, whilst others label the largest muscles. Alternatively, the task could be differentiated by giving additional labels which are not relevant as a distraction to the more able learners. The number of labels could also be increased or decreased, or more difficult terminology used.

> ### Tip
>
> If learners are creating their own labels, use sticky or post-it notes as they are easy to remove. If you are using a person or live animal, ensure you find a safe method for labelling which will not cause them any harm or distress, such as using a chalk-based product.

## Further reading and weblinks

Higgins G (2011) *How Your Horse Moves: A Unique Visual Guide to Improving Performance*: David and Charles, Exeter.

Thought Co – *The visual learning style* – https://www.thoughtco.com/visual-learning-style-3212062

https://tinyurl.com/y9flt4jw

# 26 Learner presentation

| Individual | √ | Small group | √ | Large group | √ |
|---|---|---|---|---|---|
| Formative | √ | Summative | √ | Preparation time | 5–10 minutes |
| Informal | √ | Formal | √ | Timing | 20–30 minutes |
| British Values | * | Employability | √ | After session marking? | * |
| English | √ | Maths | * | Digital skills | * |
| Entry Level | | Level 1 and 2 | √ | Level 3 upwards | √ |

*depends upon what and how you are planning to use the approach*

## What is it?

Learner presentations give learners the opportunity to research, and then present their findings regarding a particular topic to their peers.

The research can form part of the session time but is better set as a homework task. The presentation should be no longer than 20 minutes (this will depend upon how many learners you have) and 10 minutes should be allowed for peer questions at the end of each one.

Depending on your group size, learners can present individually, in pairs or in small groups.

## What can it be used for?

Learner presentations are a great way to summarise a topic or subject which learners have been working towards. They are sometimes used as a formal assessment method towards the achievement of an aspect of an apprenticeship programme or a qualification. However, they can also be used informally, e.g. to introduce a new subject or topic. This would enable you to gain a starting point for each learner's skills, knowledge and understanding if they give a short presentation regarding what they know so far. You will need to be specific as to what resources are available for learners to use, and how interactive you want their presentation to be.

## Resources

- Computer and projector (if relevant)
- Flipchart and pens (if relevant)
- Other resources as needed, such as audio and visual aids

# Advantages

👍 Supports independent research, thinking and learning skills

👍 Encourages teamwork (if working in groups)

👍 Develops presentation skills and confidence

👍 Develops employability skills

# Disadvantages

👎 Can be time-consuming and easily use up time

👎 A time limit must be set for each presentation

👎 Difficult to identify who has researched what (if working in groups)

👎 Not supportive of shy learners or those lacking in confidence

# How can I measure my learners' progress, meet individual needs and demonstrate stretch and challenge for all?

Progress measures will be made via observation of the presentations and how well your learners respond to peer questioning. You may need to ask your own questions if you are unable to ascertain how much input each learner has made towards the research or to check further understanding.

By carrying out research, individuals are developing independent thinking and learning skills. Differentiating the task or question relevant to particular individual needs and levels will enable stretch and challenge.

If learners are working in pairs or small groups, you will need to consider how best to group them in terms of ability.

---

### Tip

You can plan for one or two learner presentations to be delivered over a number of sessions, rather than all the learners delivering their presentation during one session.

---

# Further reading and weblinks

Gravells A (2017) *Principles and Practices of Teaching and Training*: Learning Matters/Sage, London.

Petty G (2009) *Evidence-based Teaching: A Practical Approach* (2nd edn): Nelson Thornes, Cheltenham.

# 27 Live lecture

| Individual | √ | Small group | √ | Large group | √ |
|---|---|---|---|---|---|
| Formative | √ | Summative | | Preparation time | 30 minutes plus |
| Informal | √ | Formal | √ | Timing | 20–60 minutes |
| British Values | * | Employability | * | After session marking? | |
| English | √ | Maths | * | Digital skills | * |
| Entry Level | * | Level 1 and 2 | √ | Level 3 upwards | √ |

*depends upon what and how you are planning to use the approach

## What is it?

A live lecture is a verbal presentation given by the teacher to their learners. It is often supported by visual aids and slides, e.g. a PowerPoint presentation, and may be followed up with a question-and-answer session.

Generally it is teacher led with little opportunity for the learners to participate. Often the live lecture is visually or aurally recorded. This is to enable the learners to access it later via a learning platform such as Moodle. Technology can be used to enable learner participation, e.g. using voting buttons for pre-set questions (see Chapter 30: Online quizzes, discussions and surveys).

## What can it be used for?

A live lecture can be formal or informal (without learner participation or some learner participation) and is a good way to present a large amount of information to a lot of learners. However, it is useful to follow it up with other activities, e.g. a workshop, to check learners' knowledge and understanding.

It might be possible to stream the live lecture in real time via the use of technology, to enable learners to see it who cannot attend in person.

## Resources

- A suitable room with seating that allows all learners to see you (and the screen if using presentation equipment)
- Computer or device with projector, or interactive whiteboard (if using technology)

- A recording device (if you wish for learners to access the lecture again afterwards)
- Supporting handouts (if required)

# Advantages

👍 Able to cover a large amount of information in one session

👍 Ability to present to a large number of learners at the same time

👍 Able to record the live lecture for future use which can be added to a learning platform, e.g. a virtual learning environment

👍 Appeals to learners whose preferred style of learning is listening

# Disadvantages

👎 Handouts can become a distraction if used (alternatively they can be given out at the end of the session or accessed electronically)

👎 Little participation is required from the learners, which might result in some becoming disengaged or disruptive

👎 Information presented can be quickly forgotten by the learner

👎 Not all learners learn at the same pace or have the same starting point of knowledge and understanding

👎 Difficult to measure progress or for learners to demonstrate stretch and challenge

👎 Reliant on the technology working (if using PowerPoint or similar)

👎 Learners may need to take notes and therefore miss an important point

👎 Teacher needs to be an effective communicator, speak loudly or use a microphone when talking to a large group

# How can I measure my learners' progress, meet individual needs and demonstrate stretch and challenge for all?

Leaving enough time at the end of the live lecture will enable you to ask questions to check and measure progress, if the group is not too large. The questions can be differentiated for each learner, perhaps by level or the use of language, to demonstrate stretch and challenge.

Larger groups of learners can complete a questionnaire at the end of the lecture identifying the key points they have learnt. This will support you in measuring their progress. Their answers could be followed up in a workshop which stretches and challenges individuals, and ensures they have increased their knowledge and understanding.

> **Tip**
>
> Always have a backup plan if you are relying on technology, e.g. a hard copy of a visual presentation. Having a drink of water close by helps to prevent your voice drying up.

## Further reading and weblinks

Exley K and Dennick R (2009) *Giving a Lecture*: Routledge, Abingdon.

Ted – *How to make a great presentation* – https://tinyurl.com/yca9h22d

# 28 Mind mapping

| Individual | √ | Small group | √ | Large group | √ |
|---|---|---|---|---|---|
| Formative | √ | Summative | | Preparation time | 5–10 minutes |
| Informal | √ | Formal | | Timing | 10–20 minutes |
| British Values | * | Employability | * | After session marking? | * |
| English | √ | Maths | * | Digital skills | * |
| Entry Level | √ | Level 1 and 2 | √ | Level 3 upwards | √ |

*depends upon what and how you are planning to use the approach

## What is it?

Mind mapping is an activity to create a diagram which helps learners organise and represent knowledge regarding a particular topic or subject.

Learners (on their own, in pairs or small groups) write or draw a topic or subject as a main heading in the centre of a blank piece of paper, and then draw a box or a circle round it, e.g. causes of global warming. They then add their knowledge of the subject by drawing branches off the main heading and adding text or drawings (in a box or circle) which link to the main heading, e.g. car emissions, burning fuels and plastic bags. Learners should be given 10 to 15 minutes to complete the mind map.

Learners should be encouraged to identify between six and eight branches which spontaneously reflect their first thoughts, focusing on the main heading only and keeping the branches in a radial structure. Using coloured pens will help to inspire the learners to be creative, but is not essential. Alternatively, learners could use a drawing device to create their mind map electronically.

Once learners have completed their mind maps, a short group discussion or paired activity should be held to check and correct any misconceptions.

## What can it be used for?

Mind mapping is a creative activity but is often biased towards the learner. However, it is a powerful tool to develop visual processing and concentration skills. It encourages learners to identify connections to a topic or subject. It also enables them to focus on the essential facts by simple labelling in boxes, rather than reading or writing lots of text.

It's an ideal activity to use at the start of a module or unit as an initial assessment to measure what learners already know. Alternatively, it can be used at the start of a session as a recap from the previous session, where learners build a map that visually represents information that they remember.

## Resources

- Paper and coloured pens, or suitable electronic devices

## Advantages

👍 Helps learners generate new ideas

👍 Supports learners to communicate ideas and thoughts

## Disadvantages

👎 Less visual or creative learners may struggle to engage with the activity

## How can I measure my learners' progress, meet individual needs and demonstrate stretch and challenge for all?

As learners create their mind maps, they are starting with knowledge, perceptions and ideas they already know, making it an ideal tool to measure progress.

When discussing the learners' mind maps, you can identify what they do not understand and target those individuals with feedback. This will help them evaluate and recognise what they need to do to develop further, thus meeting their individual needs and demonstrating stretch and challenge.

> ### Tip
>
> Once learners have mastered mind mapping, they can progress to concept mapping (see Chapter 11) to stretch and challenge them further.

## Further reading and weblinks

Buzan T (2008) *Mind Maps for Kids – Study Skills*: HarperCollins, London.

Inspiration Software. INC – *Teaching and learning with mind maps* – https://tinyurl.com/n5hk4oh

# 29 Newspaper article or blog

| Individual | √ | Small group | √ | Large group | √ |
|---|---|---|---|---|---|
| Formative | √ | Summative | √ | Preparation time | 10 minutes |
| Informal | √ | Formal | √ | Timing | 30–60 minutes |
| British Values | * | Employability | * | After session marking? | √ |
| English | √ | Maths | * | Digital skills | * |
| Entry Level | | Level 1 and 2 | √ | Level 3 upwards | √ |

*depends upon what and how you are planning to use the approach

## What is it?

Newspaper articles or blogs is an activity which enables learners to read examples which relate to the current topic or subject, and then write their own.

Alternatively, learners could read something and then re-write it in their own words to demonstrate their understanding of it.

You could ask your learners to write from a particular perspective, e.g. positive or negative, or to be unbiased. This activity can be individual or you could place learners in pairs or groups of four to six.

## What can it be used for?

Writing a newspaper article/blog is a splendid way for learners to summarise a topic or subject which they have been working towards. It can be used as a formal assessment method towards the achievement of an aspect of the programme or qualification. Alternatively, it can also be used informally to develop knowledge and understanding in relation to the topic or subject, and support the development of research and creative writing skills. A time limit should be given for completion.

The marking and assessment of the newspaper article/blog will help you identify any difficulties a learner might be having regarding the topic or subject.

A discussion should be held at the end of the activity where learners should be encouraged to identify two or three key learning points.

# Resources

- Access to subject-related newspaper articles/blogs
- Paper and pens (or electronic devices) for noting down findings and ideas
- Printer (if the articles/blogs are not accessible electronically)

# Advantages

- Supports independent research, thinking and learning skills
- Can be adapted to use as individual, paired work or for small groups
- Can be created, completed and accessed electronically
- Can challenge a learner's potential
- Encourages teamwork (if working in pairs or groups)
- Develops research and creative writing skills

# Disadvantages

- Can be time-consuming and easily use up time (alternatively, it could be set as a home-work task)
- Difficult to identify who has researched what (if working in pairs or groups)
- Can be time-consuming to plan, assess, and to provide individual feedback
- Can cause some learners to feel anxious and overwhelmed
- If set as a homework task it can be difficult to know if it is the learner's own work (an authenticity statement could be signed by the learner)

# How can I measure my learners' progress, meet individual needs and demonstrate stretch and challenge for all?

Progress will be measured by assessing the completed newspaper article/blog. The feed-back you give should be developmental and constructive, not just descriptive, i.e. such as *well done* which doesn't help the learner know how to develop and improve. You could also give feedback regarding spelling, grammar and punctuation, as well as the content.

The activity can be differentiated by word count, e.g. a higher-level learner could have a word count of 1000 words, whereas a lower level learner could have a word count of 700 words. Alternatively, you could give a list of expected content to be covered, or technical words to be included in the newspaper article/blog.

Progress can also be measured by a group discussion regarding how the learners approached the activity and what they learnt as a result.

> **Tip**
>
> This activity can be adapted to use on learning platforms such as a virtual learning environment (VLE), as an extension activity or as homework.

# Further reading and weblinks

Gravells A (2017) *Principles and Practices of Teaching and Training*: Learning Matters/Sage, London.

Scholastic – *Writing a newspaper article* – https://tinyurl.com/y7yx5vmt

# 30 Online quizzes, discussions and surveys

| Individual | √ | Small group | √ | Large group | √ |
|---|---|---|---|---|---|
| Formative | √ | Summative | | Preparation time | 30 minutes plus |
| Informal | √ | Formal | | Timing | 30–60 minutes |
| British Values | * | Employability | * | After session marking? | |
| English | √ | Maths | * | Digital skills | √ |
| Entry Level | √ | Level 1 and 2 | √ | Level 3 upwards | √ |

*depends upon what and how you are planning to use the approach

## What is it?

Online quizzes, discussions and surveys are fun ways to consolidate learning, either individually or in groups.

They can be accessed via an interactive game-based learning platform which enables you to devise your own activities by using online apps. Examples are Kahoot! Socrative, GoogleDocs and Plickers. You can search for these online, or key in *online quizzes* to a search engine to find them.

You can devise your own questions for the quiz or plan to use a discussion or a survey. Discussions could also take place via closed social media groups either outside of or during the session.

You can also add video clips and images to make these more engaging or download ready-made material. Learners can answer the questions using their own devices, e.g. their smart phones.

## What can it be used for?

It can be used to reinforce learning and understanding, as a formative assessment activity, or to re-engage learners. It can be used at the end of a session to gain feedback, as a poll or a survey.

It works very well on an interactive whiteboard which all learners can see, with them using their own devices to answer the questions. It can also be used as a distance learning tool as learners can participate from home or other environments.

# Resources required

- A good reliable internet connection
- Devices with internet access for the learners to use such as their smart phones
- An interactive whiteboard (if available)

# Advantages

👍 Works on most devices which have a reliable internet connection

👍 No account or login by the learners is required

👍 It's engaging and supports social learning

👍 Most online apps are free to use

👍 Can make learning fun

👍 Great for learners who are usually unwilling to participate in group work

# Disadvantages

👎 Reliance on an internet connection

👎 Learners need a device to participate

👎 Time-consuming to set up

👎 Can cause too much competitiveness

👎 Can seem trivial to some learners

👎 Learners may need to use their own mobile data if they are unable to connect to wi-fi

# How can I measure my learners' progress, meet individual needs and demonstrate stretch and challenge for all?

Setting online quizzes as homework tasks or extension activities will enable you to send learners different links at different levels to meet their individual needs. Playing the quiz a second time enables learners to try and beat their own score, and demonstrates their progress.

Shortening time limits to answer the questions (as the learners progress through them) will support them in preparing for exams (i.e. to between 5 and 120 seconds for each question).

Learners can also be encouraged to create their own quizzes to deepen knowledge and understanding, and then give them to their peers to answer.

A peer-led discussion after the quiz will help you identify progress, or you could set up a survey or a poll asking individual learners to vote or comment, e.g. 'How confident are you feeling about your understanding of …?'. Learners can discuss as a group, add comments to the survey, or if you add a scale (e.g. I not at all confident, 2 fairly confident, or 3 very confident) learners can vote.

---

### Tip

By using the vote option, you can introduce British Values and the rule of democracy. A discussion could take place about why people vote in a certain way, and how the results have an impact.

---

## Further reading and weblinks

Google Docs – *Creating a quiz in Google Documents* – https://tinyurl.com/y8g7uqtd

Kahoot! – *What is Kahoot!* – https://tinyurl.com/yas8lp25

Online Tools – *Plickers* – https://tinyurl.com/ya7vs2kl

Socrative – *Meet Socrative* – https://tinyurl.com/y92qk5q9

# 31  Optimists and pessimists

| Individual | | Small group | √ | Large group | √ |
|---|---|---|---|---|---|
| Formative | √ | Summative | | Preparation time | 10 minutes |
| Informal | √ | Formal | | Timing | 15–30 minutes |
| British Values | √ | Employability | √ | After session marking? | |
| English | √ | Maths | * | Digital skills | |
| Entry Level | | Level 1 and 2 | √ | Level 3 upwards | √ |

*depends upon what and how you are planning to use the approach

## What is it?

Optimists and pessimists is an activity which enables learners to discuss the different sides of something.

Learners are given five minutes to read a text related to the current topic or subject. After reading the text, a short group discussion should be held regarding the meaning of an optimist and the meaning of a pessimist. A good analogy is the glass half full or the glass half empty, i.e. an optimist sees the glass as half full, a pessimist sees it as half empty.

The whole group is divided into two and half the learners are given five minutes to reread the text and note down key optimistic points. The other half of the group are asked to carry out the same activity but to note down key pessimistic points. Learners are then asked to pair up with a peer from the opposite side and discuss and debate their findings. This could be followed up with the snowballing activity (see Chapter 39).

The whole activity should be repeated with different text, and with learners swapping roles.

## What can it be used for?

This is a great activity to use when learners have a lot of written text to understand. It gives them the opportunity to read the text and take on a positive or a negative role before sharing with their peers. In addition, by listening to the opposing point of view and discussing and debating as a whole group, learners are able to consider alternative views, supporting the development of employability skills.

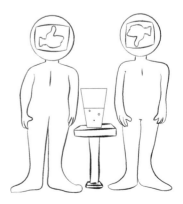

It is ideal for summarising a topic or a subject which learners have been working towards.

The optimist and pessimist activity is also a fantastic tool to develop the learners' *Affective* domain which is part of Bloom's Taxonomies of Learning (1956).

## Resources

* Topic or subject-related written text
* Paper and pens (or electronic devices) for noting down findings and ideas

## Advantages

👍 Develops speaking and listening skills

👍 Helps increase learner confidence and self-esteem

👍 Demonstrates understanding

👍 Can be engaging and active for most learners

👍 Encourages learners to collaborate through social learning

👍 Encourages learners to embrace British Values through respect for each other and for different points of view

## Disadvantages

👎 A shy, less confident learner may struggle to engage with the activity

👎 Some learners might dominate, or become loud if the groups are not managed effectively throughout the activity

## How can I measure my learners' progress, meet individual needs and demonstrate stretch and challenge for all?

Progress measures will be made through observation of the activity and listening to the learners sharing their findings.

You may need to ask your own questions of the learners at the end of the activity to check knowledge and understanding. This will also give you the opportunity to stretch and challenge each individual to their full potential.

Differentiating the written text to suit different abilities and levels will support you to meet individual needs.

> **Tip**
>
> To develop independent skills, you could ask your learners to read and research the text, prior to attending the session. This would allow more time within the session for the discussion and debate.

# Further reading and weblinks

Bloom BS (1956) *Taxonomy of Educational Objectives – The Classification of Educational Goals*: McKay, New York.

History of Education – *Taxonomy of education objectives* – https://tinyurl.com/y6vxgnqr

Teach the Earth – *What is the Affective Domain anyway?* – https://tinyurl.com/ybo3326g

# 32 Peer review

| Individual | | Small group | √ | Large group | √ |
|---|---|---|---|---|---|
| Formative | √ | Summative | | Preparation time | 20 minutes plus |
| Informal | √ | Formal | | Timing | 40–60 minutes |
| British Values | * | Employability | * | After session marking? | * |
| English | √ | Maths | * | Digital skills | |
| Entry Level | | Level 1 and 2 | √ | Level 3 upwards | √ |

*depends upon what and how you are planning to use the approach*

## What is it?

Peer review is an activity where learners follow set criteria to apply to their own work, and then follow the same criteria to review each other's work. It enables them to learn from each other. For example, you could set a homework task of a written assignment giving learners clear guidance on what criteria they should meet, a word count and the date they should bring their completed work to your session. On the day they bring the assignment in, they should swap their work with a peer and be given ten minutes to read through each other's work. Next, they should sit with their peer and for ten minutes, verbally feedback on their findings which should include:

- what they found interesting
- what could be improved
- one thing they will use in their own work.

Learners are then given twenty minutes to make any amendments or improvements to their own work. This can be handed in to you for checking.

## What can it be used for?

Peer review can be used to formatively assess written, verbal or practical activities. It increases learners' responsibility and can give them independence. It helps to develop a learner's understanding towards the intended outcomes, and supports thinking and listening skills. Learners need to be aware in advance that it is going to happen.

## Resources

- An assignment or task with set criteria or identified outcomes

# Advantages

👍 Supports learners to understand the required criteria or outcomes

👍 Develops evaluation skills

👍 Promotes responsibility and independence

👍 Supports thinking and listening skills

👍 Provides an opportunity for learners to learn from each other

# Disadvantages

👎 Can be subjective as peer pressure may affect the feedback given, e.g. some learners might not get on, therefore you will need to be careful how you pair them

👎 Learners may not understand how to know if the criteria have been met

👎 Can be time-consuming

👎 Some learners may not want to engage in the activity

# How can I measure my learners' progress, meet individual needs and demonstrate stretch and challenge for all?

Assignments or tasks should be set at the appropriate level to which the learner is already working. This will enable you to meet individual needs by differentiation of the criteria to a higher level, to demonstrate stretch and challenge.

You should plan who will review each other's work prior to the activity by matching learner needs, e.g. you may decide to pair lower level learners together and higher level learners together as they have completed the same criteria, or a higher level learner with a lower level learner to encourage peer learning.

Observing and listening to the learners feeding back to each other will enable you to measure the progress they have made in developing their understanding of the required criteria. If you have time, you can also assess their final written work.

> ### Tip
>
> Design a peer review template that learners can complete during the peer review activity. This could include the criteria or outcomes which are being assessed, along with the three bullet points listed under *What is it?*

# Further reading and weblinks

The Teaching Centre – *Planning and guiding in-class peer review* – https://tinyurl.com/yyovcyeu

University of Exeter – *Peer and self assessment in student work: principles and criteria* – https://tinyurl.com/y3g5papt

# 33    Picture prompt

| Individual | √ | Small group | √ | Large group | √ |
|---|---|---|---|---|---|
| Formative | √ | Summative | | Preparation time | 30 minutes plus |
| Informal | √ | Formal | | Timing | 20–30 minutes |
| British Values | * | Employability | * | After session marking? | |
| English | * | Maths | * | Digital skills | |
| Entry Level | √ | Level 1 and 2 | √ | Level 3 upwards | √ |

*depends upon what and how you are planning to use the approach

## What is it?

Picture prompt is an activity to enable learners to find out information regarding an image. It can be an individual, paired or group activity.

Learners are given an image related to the current topic or subject, with no explanation. The learners must identify what the image is, research it and explain it. For example, a motor engineering learner could be given an image of an engine part which they must first recognise and name correctly, followed by explaining how it works. Or a group of drama learners could be given an image and asked to discuss for 10 minutes what is happening in the image. Next, they are asked to role play to their peers what they have identified from the image.

The activity can be verbal or written depending on the needs of your learners. A group discussion should be held at the end of the activity to identify key learning points.

## What can it be used for?

Picture prompt encourages learners to undertake research, fact find, generate new ideas and make decisions. It can be used individually to support research and decision making, and if used with groups it can encourage teamwork.

It can be included during any point in a session to refocus learners or set as an extension activity or homework task. Picture prompt can be used for theory or practical topics or subjects.

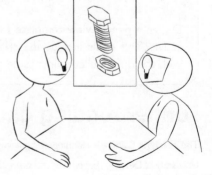

## Resources

- Access to a range of topic or subject-related images (hard copy or digital)

# Advantages

👍 Supports active learning

👍 Visually stimulating

👍 Supports memory recall

# Disadvantages

👎 Can be difficult to collate appropriate clear images

👎 Time-consuming to set up initially (but can be used for future groups)

# How can I measure my learners' progress, meet individual needs and demonstrate stretch and challenge for all? (A heading)

Learner progress is measured at the end of this activity by the learners' findings and their explanations relating to the identification of the image, and the research they have undertaken. If learners have been asked to write down their findings, marking and assessment of their work will enable you to identify individual progress. If learners have been asked to verbally explain the image, you will have an immediate progress measure. In addition, asking related questions will support stretching and challenging individuals.

Images should be differentiated and chosen according to each learner's ability. This is to ensure learning needs are met and to allow individuals to demonstrate stretch and challenge to their full potential.

> **Tip**
>
> Picture prompt is a great tool to develop learners' creative writing skills. You could ask them to write a certain number of words in a given time, then pair the learners to read and discuss each other's response.

# Further reading and weblinks

BBC Bitesize – *Descriptive writing* – http://tinyurl.com/y38uacqo

Theatrefolk – *Picture Prompt: What are they talking about?*
https://tinyurl.com/y8n4z4tb

# 34   Quescussion

| Individual | | Small group | √ | Large group | √ |
|---|---|---|---|---|---|
| Formative | √ | Summative | | Preparation time | 5–10 minutes |
| Informal | √ | Formal | | Timing | 30–45 minutes |
| British Values | √ | Employability | * | After session marking? | |
| English | √ | Maths | * | Digital skills | * |
| Entry Level | | Level 1 and 2 | √ | Level 3 upwards | √ |

*depends upon what and how you are planning to use the approach*

## What is it?

A quescussion is a discussion through the use of questions only. The teacher first asks a question related to a particular topic. Learners must respond or add to the discussion in the form of more questions. The initial question will not get answered, however it enables learners to develop their knowledge, understanding and confidence regarding the topic.

There are two rules:

1. Only questions are allowed.
2. If someone answers in any format other than a question, they cannot participate again until four other people have spoken using a question.

Depending on your group, learners can take turns or just shout out their question.

A five-minute discussion can be held at the end of the session to discuss any misconceptions or queries.

## What can it be used for?

It's a great way to introduce learners to a new or controversial topic, allowing them to ask questions without directly stating their own view. The questions can be formally written on the board or flipchart paper by the teacher, or by the learners to develop their confidence and literacy skills.

## Resources

• A way to record/note learners' questions

# Advantages

👍 Enables learners to generate a wide variety of thoughts

👍 Great for introducing a new or controversial subject

👍 Can be used to develop literacy skills

👍 Can be used to bring in British Values in terms of democracy

👍 Can determine levels of knowledge and understanding

# Disadvantages

👎 Can soon get very loud if not fully managed

👎 Assumes learners are confident to engage in a discussion using questions

👎 Learners need to understand the difference between a question and a statement, e.g. 'Small groups are easier to manage than large groups, aren't they?'. This is a statement not a question. The question could be 'How can you manage a large group?'.

👎 Teacher must ensure all learners participate

# How can I measure my learners' progress, meet individual needs and demonstrate stretch and challenge for all?

Observation of the learners and the questions they ask can help you measure their knowledge and understanding.

Rather than use it as a whole group activity, you could differentiate the learners into smaller groups and let them note down their own questions. These can be shared and discussed with the whole group at the end of the activity. Alternatively, you could ask your learners to answer the questions after everyone has taken a turn.

To stretch and challenge learners further, you could focus them on two or three of the key questions raised, in greater depth.

Alternatively, if the questions are written on a whiteboard or flipchart paper, the learners can vote on the question that they would like to explore. This enables you to embed British Values of rules of democracy. Voting could take place electronically if the equipment enables this (see Chapter 30 – Online quizzes, discussions and surveys).

> **Tip**
>
> If you have a particularly loud or boisterous group, ask the learners to note down the question on paper and hold it up above their head without speaking. This is known as silent quescussion.

# Further reading and weblinks

Dhand H (2005) *Techniques of Teaching*: Ashish Publishers, Ladakh.

Petty G (2009) *Evidence-based Teaching: A Practical Approach* (2nd edn): Nelson Thornes, Cheltenham.

# 35 Question bowl

| Individual | √ | Small group | √ | Large group | √ |
|---|---|---|---|---|---|
| Formative | √ | Summative | | Preparation time | 30 minutes plus |
| Informal | √ | Formal | | Timing | 20–45 minutes |
| British Values | * | Employability | * | After session marking? | |
| English | √ | Maths | * | Digital skills | * |
| Entry Level | √ | Level 1 and 2 | √ | Level 3 upwards | √ |

*depends upon what and how you are planning to use the approach*

## What is it?

The question bowl activity is a way of enabling learners to learn from each other.

You will need a bank of written, open questions related to a topic or subject, with varying levels of difficulty. The questions are folded (so they are not visible) and placed in a bowl or a box. Learners can work as individuals, pairs or small groups, but ideally with no more than six in a group.

The learner (or one learner from the pair or group) draws one question out of the bowl, reads it out, and must answer the question correctly to gain a point. If the learner answers the question incorrectly, they miss a turn and the question is passed on to the next person, pair or group. They must then answer the original question correctly before drawing another question, giving them a chance to earn two points if they answer both questions correctly.

A question which has been answered incorrectly should be passed round the learners, giving everyone an opportunity to answer. If no one can answer the question correctly, it should be put to one side and revisited after the activity.

The activity continues until every learner, pair or group has attempted to answer a certain number of questions, i.e. six. The winner is the one(s) with the most points. You can decide how many questions are used based on the time you have.

## What can it be used for?

Question bowl is a fantastic tool to support learners to revise and recap. It's ideally used as practice before an exam by the use of sample exam questions. It can also be used to start a session to check learning from a previous session or at the end of a session as a summary.

If you have time towards the end of a session, you could ask your learners to each write a question (and separately note down a suitable response) which could be used as a closing activity. As there probably won't be time to use all the questions, some could be carried over to become a starter activity for the next session to refresh knowledge.

## Resources

- A bank of written questions
- A bowl or box to store the questions in
- A resource to record the scores (this can be electronic, a whiteboard or paper based)

## Advantages

👍 Enables the learner to think about what they are learning

👍 Challenges a learner's potential

👍 A fun and effective way of testing knowledge and understanding

👍 Can be used at any point during the session

👍 Re-focuses groups

👍 Re-engages individuals

👍 Can be differentiated to meet individual needs

## Disadvantages

👎 Questions must be *open* otherwise you will only gain a *yes* or *no* response which doesn't demonstrate knowledge or understanding

👎 Questions must be unambiguous

👎 A shy or nervous learner may not engage well in this activity as they may struggle to answer in front of their peers (groups or teams could alleviate this)

👎 Some learners may shout out and try to answer each other's questions

👎 Difficult to manage with a large group of learners

👎 If using the activity in pairs or small groups, it's difficult to know who has engaged in answering the question

👎 Learners may become too competitive

👎 Time-consuming to set up (but can be used again with other learners)

# How can I measure my learners' progress, meet individual needs and demonstrate stretch and challenge for all?

Using the question bowl will enable you to measure a learner's progress by their answer. Using different coloured card or paper to write differentiated questions on will help to meet individual needs and demonstrate stretch and challenge, e.g. use blue card for learners who are undertaking a GCSE foundation paper and yellow card for learners undertaking a GCSE high paper. Alternatively you could have two bowls of questions and let learners choose which bowl to take a question from, i.e. easy or hard.

---

### Tip

Ask learners to keep the scores to help develop their maths skills.

---

# Further reading and weblinks

Petty G (2009) *Evidence-based Teaching: A Practical Approach* (2nd edn): Nelson Thornes, Cheltenham.

Your dictionary – *Examples of open-ended and closed-ended questions* – https://tinyurl.com/ybc2pm9g

# 36 Rhyme and rap

| Individual | | Small group | √ | Large group | √ |
|---|---|---|---|---|---|
| Formative | √ | Summative | | Preparation time | 5 minutes |
| Informal | √ | Formal | | Timing | 20–30 minutes |
| British Values | * | Employability | * | After session marking? | |
| English | √ | Maths | * | Digital skills | |
| Entry Level | * | Level 1 and 2 | √ | Level 3 upwards | √ |

*depends upon what and how you are planning to use the approach

## What is it?

Rhyme and rap is an activity which requires learners to be imaginative by creating their own phrases or songs to help them remember key points.

Learners are divided into groups of three to six and given five to ten minutes to create a short rhyme, rap or verse. This should be related to the current topic or subject and will be shared with the whole group. For example, the *Dem Bones* song: *The toe bone connected to the foot bone, the foot bone connected to the ankle bone, the ankle bone connected to the leg bone* etc. Another example is the *Month* rhyme: *30 days has September, April, June and November, all the rest have 31 except February alone.* The learners should then share their creation with the whole group.

## What can it be used for?

It's a fun way to aid learners' memory and recall, particularly before an exam when they have to remember a sequence of something, or the meaning of a technical word. It's also a brilliant activity to use part way through a session to check learning and re-engage learners. Although it might work best with small groups, individual learners could create their own and then share with a partner.

## Resources

* Paper and pens (or electronic devices) for noting down findings and ideas

## Advantages

👍 Aids memory recall

👍 Is fun and encourages creativity

👍 Encourages teamwork and collaboration

# Disadvantages

👎 Can be time-consuming

👎 Not all learners may want or be able to participate

👎 Some learners may get too dramatic

# How can I measure my learners' progress, meet individual needs and demonstrate stretch and challenge for all?

Knowing the learners' starting points, and grouping the learners, is key to meeting individual needs, e.g. learners who are taking a Level Two General Massage programme and are currently working on a basic massage routine, will be able to recall it easily, whereas others who are not, won't. The learners who are unable to recall the routine should be given a script with the massage moves on, and asked to make a rhyme or rap to help them remember it. The learners who already know the routine could be asked to create a rhyme or rap of the basic routine, but to include some advanced techniques. This will also demonstrate stretch and challenge.

Walking around the groups during the activity and observing the learners will help you measure individual progress. You will need to correct any mistakes prior to the learners sharing their creations with the whole group, otherwise those learners might remember the incorrect version. It's also a good opportunity to check spelling and grammar.

> ### Tip
>
> Once the learners have shared their creation, let the whole group choose their favourite one and use it at the start of the next session as a group recap activity.

# Further reading and weblinks

Gravells A (2017) *Principles and Practices of Teaching and Training*: Learning Matters/Sage, London.

ManiaTales interactive imagination – *Rhythm and rhymes empower memory & learning* – http://tinyurl.com/y6edjthf

# 37 Role play

| Individual | | Small group | √ | Large group | |
|---|---|---|---|---|---|
| Formative | √ | Summative | | Preparation time | 5–10 minutes |
| Informal | √ | Formal | | Timing | * |
| British Values | * | Employability | √ | After session marking? | |
| English | * | Maths | * | Digital skills | |
| Entry Level | √ | Level 1 and 2 | √ | Level 3 upwards | √ |

*depends upon what and how you are planning to use the approach

## What is it?

Role play is a technique which allows learners to explore different situations which they may encounter in real life, but in a realistic and supportive environment. It enables them to develop skills and strategies which will help them in the future, by assuming the role of another person, or acting out a scenario or hypothetical situation.

Depending on the topic or subject, it can take anything between 20 minutes to three hours. For example, if you wish your learners to role play how to manage an angry customer, the activity would take 10 minutes followed by a discussion and feedback. If your learners are developing skills such as assuming the role of a salon manager in a hairdressing realistic working environment, it could take two to three hours.

## What can it be used for?

It's a marvellous way to develop learners' confidence and skills in a supported environment. Role play is designed to enable the development of problem-solving skills and to put learning into practice. It can be used in any suitable environment or workshop to act out a situation or scenario, or in a realistic working environment to develop employability skills. Clear roles and time limits will need to be defined.

Pairs or small groups of learners could act out a scenario and be observed by their peers, who could then ask questions and/or give feedback. This would help develop their observation, questioning and communication skills.

## Resources

- A realistic working environment if you are developing skills for employment
- A classroom or workshop if you are developing communication and problem-solving skills

# Advantages

👍 Enables hands-on practice to apply new skills in a safe, supported and realistic setting

👍 Allows decision making and problem solving

👍 Develops understanding from a different perspective

👍 Demonstrates current skill levels

👍 Links theory to practice

# Disadvantages

👎 Can be difficult to engage learners who are easily embarrassed or shy

👎 Can quickly become disorganised if not kept under control

👎 Difficult to keep all learners engaged at the same time

👎 Not all learners will take it seriously

# How can I measure my learners' progress, meet individual needs and demonstrate stretch and challenge for all?

Observing the learners undertaking their roles will enable you to see them demonstrate their current skills, knowledge and understanding. You can judge whether they have made progress from their starting point, and how they react in different situations.

Each role should be carefully planned to support individual needs and ensure stretch and challenge.

A short reflective activity should be completed after the role play which enables learners to identify at least one thing they would do differently, based on their experience.

---

### Tip

Ensure all learners fully understand their role and the purpose of the activity. Agree ground rules prior to the start of the activity to prevent any inappropriate behaviour.

---

# Further reading and weblinks

British Council – *Role-Play* – https://tinyurl.com/yytor9k3

Gravells A (2017) *Principles and Practices of Teaching and Training*: Learning Matters/Sage, London.

# 38 Simulation

| Individual | √ | Small group | √ | Large group | √ |
|---|---|---|---|---|---|
| Formative | √ | Summative | √ | Preparation time | 15–20 minutes |
| Informal | √ | Formal | √ | Timing | * |
| British Values | * | Employability | √ | After session marking? | |
| English | * | Maths | * | Digital skills | * |
| Entry Level | √ | Level 1 and 2 | √ | Level 3 upwards | √ |

*depends upon what and how you are planning to use the approach

## What is it?

Simulation is an imitation activity, carried out when the real activity would be too dangerous for the learner to undertake. It is a form of experiential learning which is learner centred, and it promotes learners' critical thinking and problem-solving skills.

The simulation allows learners to demonstrate in a safe and supported environment, what they might do in a real situation. For the simulation to work, it is vital that the activity chosen reflects real practice and genuine situations.

## What can it be used for?

Simulation is often used to prepare learners for employment and is ideal practice in a realistic working environment (RWE). For example, a forensic science learner may practise their skills in a simulated crime scene. They are able to carry out fingerprint analysis, DNA analysis, and collect samples and materials relating to a simulated crime. Or a nervous trainee vet nurse could practise injecting an orange before injecting a live animal such as a horse. The orange helps the learner feel how much pressure to use to penetrate the peel which is similar to horse skin, without injury to the learner or the animal.

Simulation is a great tool for preparing learners for interviews as it enables them to go through the process of an interview in a supportive environment.

## Resources

- Specialist equipment (depending on the simulation)
- A suitable environment

# Advantages

👍 Helps the learners to develop confidence in a supportive environment

👍 Interactive and learner centered

👍 Allows the learners to safely try something out

# Disadvantages

👎 Careful planning is needed

👎 Can be time-consuming

👎 Specialist equipment may be needed

👎 Not all learners may be able to participate fully

# How can I measure my learners' progress, meet individual needs and demonstrate stretch and challenge for all?

Learner progress should be continually monitored by observation throughout the simulated activity. The simulation should be planned well in advance and the activity set at a level which meets individual needs. This will naturally allow each learner to be stretched and challenged at the appropriate pace and level, e.g. a learner taking a first-aid course may already have experience and could undertake a simulation of dealing with multiple casualties at the same time, whereas a learner with no experience would practise through simulation dealing with one casualty at a time, building up their skills and experience at their own pace.

---

### Tip

The simulation must reflect a realistic working environment otherwise the learners may not take it seriously.

---

# Further reading and weblinks

Ellington H et al. (1998) *Using Games and Simulations in the Classroom*: Kogan Page, London.

Jones K (1995) *Simulations – A Handbook for Teachers and Trainers*: Kogan Page, London.

Teaching with simulations – https://serc.carleton.edu/sp/library/simulations/index.html

# 39 Snowballing

| Individual | | Small group | √ | Large group | √ |
|---|---|---|---|---|---|
| Formative | √ | Summative | | Preparation time | 30 minutes plus |
| Informal | √ | Formal | | Timing | 30–50 minutes |
| British Values | * | Employability | * | After session marking? | |
| English | √ | Maths | * | Digital skills | * |
| Entry Level | * | Level 1 and 2 | √ | Level 3 upwards | √ |

*depends upon what and how you are planning to use the approach*

## What is it?

Snowballing is an activity which enables learners to build upon their knowledge by increasing the group size they are in.

Learners are provided with information related to the current topic or subject; this could be in the form of text, pictures, an object or a resource. Individually the learners are given five to ten minutes to read through the information or analyse the picture, object or resource. They should note down any ideas and key facts relating to the information, for sharing with their peers.

Each learner then partners with another learner and for five minutes as a pair, they share their findings and information. The pair join another pair to form a group of four and share their findings and information for five minutes. Groups continue to join each other, sharing their findings and information until the whole group is back together again and all ideas have been shared.

A whole group discussion and debate is then held to establish key facts and correct any misconceptions.

## What can it be used for?

Snowballing is a great activity to develop learners' independent thinking and learning skills. It also encourages them to work collaboratively and listen to each other's thoughts and ideas.

It can be used at the start of a session to introduce a new topic or subject, or at the end of a session as a recap. It can also be used at any point during a session as a check on progress. If you have a very large group, you could aim for two to three groups rather than one full group.

# Resources

- Topic or subject-related written information, text, pictures, objects or resources

- Paper and pens (or electronic devices) for noting down findings and ideas

# Advantages

👍 Encourages learners to collaborate through social learning

👍 Learner centered

👍 Learners are actively engaged as they have to think for themselves

👍 Helps learners to organise and structure their thoughts and ideas

👍 Supports the development of communication skills

# Disadvantages

👎 A shy, less confident learner may struggle to engage with the activity

👎 Difficult to meet all individual needs

👎 Some learners might dominate or become loud if the groups are not managed effectively throughout the activity

# How can I measure my learners' progress, meet individual needs and demonstrate stretch and challenge for all?

Careful observation of the learners' activity during the paired and group work, coupled with the whole group discussion and debate at the end of the activity, will enable you to measure learner progress.

The initial information given to the learners should be differentiated to meet individual needs, and ensure all learners are stretched and challenged. This could be grouped into higher, middle and lower. For example, higher level learners could be given in-depth written information which requires them to extract key points for sharing. Middle level learners could be given a picture which requires them to identify several key points before sharing with a partner, and lower level learners could be given an object or a resource to describe. As the learners pair up, the information shared gradually develops into the full story, making all learners' contributions important.

> **Tip**
>
> Use directed questions at the end of the whole group discussion to further stretch and challenge individuals.

# Further reading and weblinks

Gravells A (2017) *Principles and Practices of Teaching and Training*: Learning Matters/Sage, London.

Petty G (2009) *Evidence-based Teaching: A Practical Approach* (2nd edn): Nelson Thornes, Cheltenham.

Back to school – *Group work: The snowballing technique* – https://tinyurl.com/yc6keymm

# 40  Textbook challenge

| Individual | | Small group | √ | Large group | √ |
|---|---|---|---|---|---|
| Formative | √ | Summative | | Preparation time | 20–30 minutes |
| Informal | √ | Formal | | Timing | 20–30 minutes |
| British Values | * | Employability | * | After session marking? | |
| English | √ | Maths | * | Digital skills | |
| Entry Level | | Level 1 and 2 | √ | Level 3 upwards | √ |

*depends upon what and how you are planning to use the approach

## What is it?

The textbook challenge is a fast-paced activity which requires learners to race against each other to find topic or subject-related words, phrases or images in textbooks or a dictionary, in the shortest time.

Each learner is given two or three topic or subject-relevant textbooks and a dictionary, e.g. give the learners a topic or subject-related word or phrase, or ask them to locate a picture of a resource. They must search the textbooks or a dictionary to find the narrative, image, or correct spelling and meaning. The winner is the first learner to find the word, text, or image in the book, and hold it above their head at the correct page.

Alternatively, you can show an image of an item and ask them to find a word which represents it.

At the end of the activity you can ask the learners to reflect for two or three minutes, and to note down two aspects they enjoyed about the activity and two of their biggest challenges. This can be followed by a group discussion.

## What can it be used for?

The textbook challenge is a fantastic tool to support learners to revise, recap or prepare for an exam. It helps to promote learners' quick-thinking skills. It is also a great way to initially assess the way

learners use books to find information, to develop research skills or to support the correct spelling of technical words, as an alternative to using the Internet.

## Resources

- Relevant textbooks and/or dictionaries for each learner
- A list of key topic or subject-related words, phrases or images

## Advantages

👍 Challenges a learner's potential

👍 A fun and effective way of testing knowledge and understanding

👍 Can be used at any point during the session

👍 Re-focuses groups

👍 Re-engages individuals

👍 Supports learners to develop research skills using textbooks

## Disadvantages

👎 Difficult to manage with a large group of learners

👎 Difficult to differentiate and can be frustrating for some learners, e.g. learners with dyslexia may struggle when under pressure to find the correct spelling of words, and become frustrated

👎 Learners may become too competitive

👎 Not all learners will take it seriously

## How can I measure my learners' progress, meet individual needs and demonstrate stretch and challenge for all?

There are two ways to measure progress during this activity. The first measure is observation of the learners searching for the answer. The second measure is the end activity when learners discuss what they enjoyed and what they found challenging.

If you are using this activity as an initial assessment, it will help you plan any additional support an individual may need for future activities.

The activity is stretching and challenging for all learners due to its fast pace, and may not be suitable for learners with learning difficulties and/or disabilities.

Tip

If you are working with large groups of learners and you don't have enough text-books and dictionaries, split the group into teams of three or four. They can share the resources and work as a team to find the answers.

# Further reading and weblinks

Cambridge Assessment – *Why do students still need textbooks?* https://tinyurl.com/y563cnt3

Quizalize – *Top 10 classroom games* – https://tinyurl.com/yahqv9m8

# 41 Think, pair and share

| Individual | | Small group | √ | Large group | √ |
|---|---|---|---|---|---|
| Formative | √ | Summative | | Preparation time | 5–10 minutes |
| Informal | √ | Formal | | Timing | 20–40 minutes |
| British Values | * | Employability | * | After session marking? | |
| English | √ | Maths | * | Digital skills | |
| Entry Level | √ | Level 1 and 2 | √ | Level 3 upwards | √ |

*depends upon what and how you are planning to use the approach

## What is it?

Think, pair and share is a learning technique which encourages learners to think a question through, using three stages:

- Stage one – learners are given five to ten minutes to answer a question or solve a problem, and must independently think of the answer.
- Stage two – working in pairs, learners have two minutes to feed back their answer to a partner, who in turn has two minutes to feed back their own findings.
- Stage three – the pair then have a further three minutes to agree an outcome which can be shared with the whole group.

Once the outcome has been shared, learners can be given a further two or three minutes to reconvene and discuss how their thinking may have changed as a result of sharing their findings.

## What can it be used for?

It can be used to introduce a new topic or subject and it is a great way to identify a learner's starting point. It can also be used to encourage a discussion or controversial debate about a particular topic or problem part way through a subject, e.g. 'Should animals be used for testing medicines prior to being used for humans?'.

## Resources

- A question or a problem for learners to discuss and resolve

# Advantages

👍 Encourages independent thinking skills and problem solving

👍 Encourages discussion and peer support

👍 Builds confidence, listening and speaking skills

👍 Quick and easy to set up

# Disadvantages

👎 Not all learners may want to take part

👎 Requires learners to be self-motivated

# How can I measure my learners' progress, meet individual needs and demonstrate stretch and challenge for all?

Think, pair and share is designed to differentiate learning by providing time for the learner to think a question or a problem through. The first stage of the process naturally stretches learners, the third stage challenges learners as they must discuss it until they have an agreed outcome. When presenting their findings back to the whole group, concepts may change again, further challenging their thought processes and decisions.

To help measure individual progress, ensure you move around the learning environment during the activity, listening and observing the pairs during their discussion. Asking the pairs to feed their outcomes back to the whole group will support you in identifying any misconceptions, and allow you to determine individual progress.

You could ask learners at the end of the activity to write down one or two key points they have learned. They could also consider how they reacted to others' opinions and why they reached their opinions.

> **Tip**
>
> Plan to pair learners with someone they don't usually work with to stretch and challenge even further, but be sensitive to individual needs.
>
> Any misconceptions should be challenged during the paired activity.

# Further reading and weblinks

Teacher Vision – *Think, Pair, Share Cooperative Learning Strategy* – https://tinyurl.com/khsnl3v

Teacher Vision – *Teaching with cooperative learning* – https://tinyurl.com/yclcf5u2

# 42   Three-minute paper

| Individual | √ | Small group | √ | Large group | √ |
|---|---|---|---|---|---|
| Formative | √ | Summative | | Preparation time | 5 minutes |
| Informal | √ | Formal | | Timing | 20–25 minutes |
| British Values | * | Employability | * | After session marking? | * |
| English | √ | Maths | | Digital skills | * |
| Entry Level | | Level 1 and 2 | √ | Level 3 upwards | √ |

*depends upon what and how you are planning to use the approach

## What is it?

The three-minute paper is a short written activity where learners are given a question related to the current topic or subject. They must quickly and concisely write their response in three minutes.

The learners' responses can be followed up as part of the session or used as a recap in the following session. The activity should be followed by a 15 to 20-minute discussion to ensure the learners have responded appropriately.

Alternatively, for learners who are working at a higher level, you can shorten the time to one minute.

## What can it be used for?

This is a wonderful way to measure progress at the end of a session. It can also identify any difficulties a learner might be having regarding the topic or subject or their learning.

It can re-engage learners part way through a session. It also supports developing reflective thought processes, promoting spontaneous writing skills and self-confidence.

## Resources

- A relevant question
- A clock or a device with an alarm to enable learners to time the activity (or you can time it).
- Paper and pens (or electronic devices) for noting down findings and ideas

# Advantages

👍 Can be used at any point of your session to re-engage learners

👍 Does not take much planning

👍 Supports identifying individuals who are struggling with a concept

👍 Can be adapted to use as paired work or small group work

👍 Develops reflective thinking skills

👍 Promotes spontaneous writing skills and self-confidence

# Disadvantages

👎 Does not support spelling and grammar (unless a device with a spelling and grammar checker is used); you could read each response afterwards to give feedback regarding this

👎 Can cause some learners to feel anxious and under pressure

👎 Not all learners may answer the question honestly

# How can I measure my learners' progress, meet individual needs and demonstrate stretch and challenge for all?

Carefully selected questions will enable you to meet individual needs, for example the questions could be:

• What was the most important thing you learned during this session today and why was that?

• What questions remained unanswered in your mind today and why?

• The one thing that I wish I'd asked during today's session is:

• What part of today's session would you least like an exam question on?

• Summarise the content of today's session.

Individual responses will enable you to ascertain where each learner is regarding their knowledge and understanding. This will allow you to measure progress and plan differentiated activities for future sessions.

Learners who struggle with their handwriting could use an electronic device or a computer.

---

**Tip**

This activity can be adapted to use on learning platforms such as a virtual learning environment (VLE), as an extension activity or as homework. If you are not present when the learners carry out the activity, you will need to trust that they have completed it within the three minutes.

---

# Further reading and weblinks

Humber – *Teaching methods* – https://tinyurl.com/lkkkdf2

Professional Learning Board – *How can I use the Minute Paper Strategy to enhance learning in the classroom?* – https://tinyurl.com/yalpyoph

# 43  Three, two, one

| Individual | | Small group | √ | Large group | √ |
|---|---|---|---|---|---|
| Formative | √ | Summative | | Preparation time | 5 minutes |
| Informal | √ | Formal | | Timing | 20–30 minutes |
| British Values | * | Employability | * | After session marking? | |
| English | √ | Maths | * | Digital skills | |
| Entry Level | | Level 1 and 2 | √ | Level 3 upwards | √ |

*depends upon what and how you are planning to use the approach

## What is it?

Three, two, one is an activity which is designed to help learners process new reading or learning materials. It can be used after presenting new information, to recap the end of a session, or after learners have undertaken topic or subject-related reading.

The activity is in three stages:

1.  Ask your learners to write down three key facts about what they have learned.

2.  Ask your learners to write down two questions about any aspects they didn't understand or need further clarity on.

3.  Ask your learners to write down one thing they found interesting and would like to learn more about.

Ask each learner to read out their three key facts, their two questions and one thing they found interesting, to the whole group. After each learner reads out their three, two, one you should facilitate a group discussion to answer the questions.

Learners can cross off their own questions if they have already been answered, but all learners should state the three key facts and one thing they found interesting.

If you are working with a large group of learners, you could divide them into smaller groups of six to eight learners to undertake the activity, and agree the answers to the questions amongst themselves. Any questions left unanswered could be discussed as a whole group activity facilitated by you.

## What can it be used for?

Three, two, one is an activity which is a great way to recap the learning at the end of a session.

It can be used at any time during the session to encourage learners to evaluate their own learning, e.g. to check understanding part way through a topic. The activity also helps learners to develop independent thinking and learning skills, as well as reflective practice.

## Resources

- Paper and pens (or electronic devices) for noting down findings and ideas

## Advantages

👍 Helps to develop independent thinking and learning skills

👍 Is learner centered

👍 Supports learners to communicate ideas and thoughts

👍 Helps learners to enhance knowledge regarding a topic and evaluate information

👍 Quick and easy to set up

## Disadvantages

👎 Not all learners may want to take part and some might need support

👎 Requires learners to be self-motivated

## How can I measure my learners' progress, meet individual needs and demonstrate stretch and challenge for all?

You can measure learner progress in two ways: the first is the individual answers to the three, two, one activity; the second is by listening to the responses during the group discussion.

To support learners for the activity, you could give them a template with headings so that they can write underneath them. Alternatively you could display the following text on a board or screen:

- Three – Write three key facts
- Two – Write two questions you need clarity on
- One – Write one thing you found interesting and would like to learn more about

Directed questioning will enable you to further challenge the learners by differentiating the questions to meet each individual's ability.

If you are using the three, two, one activity as a recap or part way through a topic, it will also support you in planning your delivery for future sessions. The responses you receive from the learners will help you identify any adjustments that need to be made to your delivery, e.g. if most of the learners have identified the same two questions, your delivery should be adjusted to address the gap.

Tip

Depending on group needs, the three, two, one order can be changed, e.g. three aspects the learners found interesting, two key facts and one question.

# Further reading and weblinks

Facing History and Ourselves – *3-2-1* – https://tinyurl.com/y3szt3r5

The teacher's toolkit – *3-2-1* – https://tinyurl.com/og5lo79

# 44 True or false?

| Individual | √ | Small group | √ | Large group | √ |
|---|---|---|---|---|---|
| Formative | √ | Summative | | Preparation time | 5 minutes |
| Informal | √ | Formal | | Timing | 10–15 minutes |
| British Values | * | Employability | * | After session marking? | |
| English | * | Maths | * | Digital skills | |
| Entry Level | √ | Level 1 and 2 | √ | Level 3 upwards | √ |

*depends upon what and how you are planning to use the approach

## What is it?

The true or false activity is a short task where the learners have to choose if a fact about the current topic or subject is true or false.

Two designated areas should be set up in the room: one a true area and one a false area. A fact is read out to the learners and they must decide within 15 seconds if they believe it to be a true fact or a false fact, by moving to the designated area of their choice.

A short discussion should be held as to why learners believe the fact is true or false before the correct answer is given. Learners then move back to their places before the next fact is read out and the activity is repeated.

## What can it be used for?

True or false is a terrific activity for recapping, to formatively assess knowledge and understanding, as an initial assessment activity, to re-engage or to re-focus learners.

It can be used at any point during a session to measure progress and to identify any misconceptions learners may be having regarding the topic or subject. It also supports learners to make decisions. However, it's worth telling your learners that they must make their own decisions and not follow their peers.

# Resources

- A list of facts which are true or false

# Advantages

- 👍 Can be used at any point of your session to re-engage learners
- 👍 Does not take much planning
- 👍 Supports identifying individuals who are struggling with a concept
- 👍 Develops decision-making skills

# Disadvantages

- 👎 Can cause some learners to feel anxious and under pressure
- 👎 Not all learners will engage or take it seriously
- 👎 Some learners may follow the majority rather than make their own decision

# How can I measure my learners' progress, meet individual needs and demonstrate stretch and challenge for all?

Start with easy facts to enable learners to gain confidence in their own decision making, before stating more complex facts to stretch and challenge learners.

Individual responses will enable you to ascertain where each learner is regarding their knowledge and understanding. This will allow you to measure progress and plan differentiated activities in future sessions.

> ## Tip
>
> If it's the first time your learners have undertaken this activity start off with three designated areas – true, false and *I'm not sure*. This will help to develop learners' confidence as they won't feel pressured to make a decision.

# Further reading and weblinks

Gravells A (2017) *Principles and Practices of Teaching and Training*: Learning Matters/Sage, London.

Teflnet – *15 warmers and fillers for true/false tasks* – https://tinyurl.com/y2uh5utx

# 45 TV commercial

| Individual | | Small group | √ | Large group | √ |
|---|---|---|---|---|---|
| Formative | √ | Summative | | Preparation time | 15–30 minutes |
| Informal | √ | Formal | | Timing | * |
| British Values | * | Employability | √ | After session marking? | * |
| English | √ | Maths | * | Digital skills | * |
| Entry Level | √ | Level 1 and 2 | √ | Level 3 upwards | √ |

*depends upon what and how you are planning to use the approach

## What is it?

TV commercial is a fun activity where learners are divided into groups of four to six, and given a theme related to the current topic or subject.

They are given 30 minutes to plan and create a one-minute TV commercial which they will act out to their peers later in the session. Alternatively, learners could continue to plan the TV commercial as a collaborative homework task and deliver it in a later session.

Learners should take the opportunity to discuss in advance what makes a good TV commercial. They could view some online (either during the session or in advance of the session) to find out what makes them effective.

You will need to plan the order of the groups, to ensure they all have a chance to deliver the TV commercial to their peers, as well as observe the others.

The peers who are observing must score the TV commercial on a scale of 1 (lowest) to 10 (highest) regarding the following areas:

- creativity
- audience engagement
- getting the topic or subject across in a clear manner.

The scores can be written on cards which are shown after the commercial. The learners must also be prepared to justify these if questioned.

## What can it be used for?

Creating a TV commercial is a fun learning activity which helps learners to develop confidence and communication skills in a supportive learning environment.

The initial planning and creation of the TV commercial supports learners to consider the topic or subject. It deepens their knowledge and understanding by discussion, and condenses what they know into one minute. They will also develop softer skills which are useful for future employment such as teamwork, leadership and problem-solving skills.

The production of the TV commercial is designed to engage different types of learners, e.g. a quiet, shy learner may decide to work behind the scenes rather than act in the commercial, whereas a charismatic confident learner may want to take the star role. The peers acting as the audience will also develop observation, decision-making and communication skills.

One learner from each group could visually record the commercial for later viewing. They could view it in their group and score themselves, comparing the scores given to them by their peers.

Five minutes should be left at the end for a short reflective activity.

## Resources

- Paper and pens (or electronic devices) for noting down findings and ideas
- Score cards (learners could verbalise the scores)
- Access to the internet to view current TV commercials (if there is time)
- A visual recording device such as a smartphone if the commercials are to be recorded

## Advantages

- Allows decision making and problem solving which support the development of employability skills
- Develops teamwork and leadership skills
- Develops understanding from a different perspective
- Easily embarrassed or shy learners can still actively engage in the activity by taking a behind-the-scenes role
- Demonstrates current skill levels
- Links theory to practice

## Disadvantages

- Can quickly become disorganised if not kept under control
- Not all learners will take it seriously

👎 Time-consuming to set up

👎 Learners might go over time

# How can I measure my learners' progress, meet individual needs and demonstrate stretch and challenge for all?

The role chosen by each learner will support their learning needs. However, it may be necessary to pre-plan who will be in the groups to ensure the dynamics are conducive to learning, and that one learner is not going to overpower another.

Careful listening and observation of the initial 30-minute discussion will enable you to identify and correct any misconceptions. It will also ensure all learners are participating and contributing in the planning and creation of the TV commercial. This will help you to measure the progress of learners' current skills, knowledge and understanding, as well as recognising the different roles learners are forming within their teams, e.g. leadership or teamwork will both contribute to developing employability skills.

The one-minute TV commercial enables learners to demonstrate stretch and challenge when they act it out, as it shows how much research has gone into capturing the topic or subject they are portraying. Even if a learner has a behind-the-scenes role, they have still contributed to the research, creation and production of the commercial.

A short reflective activity at the end of the session will support learners to identify at least one thing they have learned based on the activity. This could be by learners writing about the experience, or verbally stating it in front of the other learners.

---

### Tip

If you are planning to run the TV commercials over a number of sessions, allow the learners to dress up in character (if possible) to emphasis the learning experience. Allow time for your learners to rehearse to make sure they keep to one minute. If you have a smaller group, the duration of the commercial could be increased.

---

# Further reading and weblinks

Gravells A (2017) *Principles and Practices of Teaching and Training*: Learning Matters/Sage, London.

ThoughtCo. – *Create a commercial* – https://tinyurl.com/ycb89rq4

# 46 Walking in your shoes

| Individual | | Small group | √ | Large group | √ |
|---|---|---|---|---|---|
| Formative | √ | Summative | | Preparation time | 5–10 minutes |
| Informal | √ | Formal | | Timing | 10–20 minutes |
| British Values | * | Employability | * | After session marking? | |
| English | √ | Maths | * | Digital skills | * |
| Entry Level | | Level 1 and 2 | √ | Level 3 upwards | √ |

*depends upon what and how you are planning to use the approach*

## What is it?

Walking in your shoes is an activity which requires the learners to deliver a short session to their peers as if they are the teacher (known as the peer-teacher).

Learners (either as an individual or in a small group) are set a homework task. Each should be given a different topic which is based on the current subject. They should read about and create some materials relating to the topics set, which they will teach to their peers in a five to ten-minute session.

The peer-teacher/s should plan and produce a variety of materials, e.g. a PowerPoint presentation, or handouts to help engage their peers.

The peer-teacher/s then deliver the session to the rest of the learners. Depending upon the size of your group, you will need to plan the order and timings carefully.

The learners must devise a few questions related to the topic as the session progresses. These should be based on the subject or material that they don't understand (a minimum of one question and a maximum of three questions).

You will need to manage the questions and resulting discussion, perhaps by nominating a few learners after each session, if the group is large. This would enable all learners to ask at least one question.

## What can it be used for?

This is a good activity which enables learners to demonstrate what they know, understand and can do. It also encourages them to start researching the next stage.

It should be used informally, and the learner/s who is/are acting as the peer-teacher/s should be urged to be as interactive as possible with their learners.

Rather than setting the activity as homework for a future session, it could be used during a session to begin talking about something new, to amalgamate learning, or to recap something.

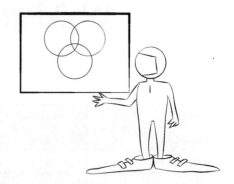

## Resources

- Access to technology if a PowerPoint or other presentation equipment is to be used
- Other resources as needed such as audio and visual aids
- Access to a printer if handouts are required

## Advantages

👍 Versatile and transferable to most subjects

👍 Learners often feel safer asking each other questions rather than asking the teacher

👍 The peer-teacher can reinforce their own learning

👍 Enables the teacher to take on the role of a facilitator

👍 Supports learners to develop presentation, communication and listening skills

👍 Supports independent research, thinking and learning skills

👍 Helps to develop leadership skills

## Disadvantages

👎 Lacks in-depth awareness of the topic or subject

👎 The peer-teacher may give out incorrect information (this could be used as a learning opportunity)

👎 Relies on the individual to be motivated to carry out the task

👎 Shy learners or those who lack confidence may struggle (learners could work in pairs or small groups to alleviate this)

👎 You will need a contingency plan in case learners are absent when they are due to present their topic

## How can I measure my learners' progress, meet individual needs and demonstrate stretch and challenge for all?

The tasks set should be differentiated to meet the needs of individual learners and to demonstrate stretch and challenge, e.g. learners studying Human Anatomy and Physiology – Skeletal Systems. Confident higher-level learners could be set a task of researching and delivering material regarding the more complex appendicular skeleton of an adult, whereas less confident and lower level learners could be set a task of researching and delivering material regarding the less complicated axial skeleton.

The peer-teacher's five to ten-minute delivery will enable you to measure their progress by observing the session and reviewing the materials used. The questions created by the learner peers in relation to the topic/subject will give you a progress measure regarding their knowledge and understanding.

---

### Tip

Learners may struggle to engage with this activity the first time you use it, as they are not teachers. They will need advice as to how to prepare and present. Persevere, as their presentation skills will improve with feedback and practice, thereby preparing them for future life challenges.

---

# Further reading and weblinks

Informed Ed – *How peer teaching improves student learning and 10 ways to encourage it* – https:// tinyurl.com/ycvh9jds

# 47 Watch, summarise and question

| Individual | | Small group | √ | Large group | √ |
|---|---|---|---|---|---|
| Formative | √ | Summative | | Preparation time | 30 minutes plus |
| Informal | √ | Formal | | Timing | 40 minutes plus |
| British Values | * | Employability | * | After session marking? | * |
| English | √ | Maths | * | Digital skills | * |
| Entry Level | | Level 1 and 2 | √ | Level 3 upwards | √ |

*depends upon what and how you are planning to use the approach

## What is it?

Watch, summarise and question is a blended learning activity which requires the learners to complete a homework task prior to the session.

Learners must watch a film or a visual recording relating to the current topic or subject as a homework task. This can be a video, DVD or something electronically accessible through a learning platform (see Chapter 17 – Flipped classroom). They are asked to make notes regarding their own key learning points immediately after they have watched it. From those notes, they should write a summary explaining their understanding of what they have watched, and then add a question based on what they have seen.

Some learners may need to watch the film or recording more than once to be able to write the summary and formulate a question.

Guidance for the question could include:

1. an aspect or concept not fully understood, or
2. something that was said or done which didn't make sense.

Learners should bring their summary and question to the next session where they are placed into groups of four to six. They can have 15 to 20 minutes to discuss the key points of the material they have seen, using their summary to explain the content to each other.

At the end of the discussion, they ask each other their question and discuss possible answers.

They must then discuss and agree one question that they can pose to the whole group, which could be a new question or any question they are not able to conclude from each other's summaries.

The group discussion should last no longer than 10 minutes and each group should pose one question.

After the activity, you should read the individual learner summaries and give constructive written feedback. This can be regarding how learners can improve their written work for the future.

# What can it be used for?

Watch, summarise and question is a fabulous activity to introduce learners to a new topic or subject prior to the session, which will allow them to explore it further during the session. The discussion and question aspect of the activity supports learners to work collaboratively to problem solve.

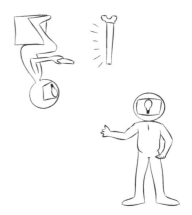

It can also be used for revision, for recapping a previous topic or to strengthen or expand on a subject previously taught.

# Resources

- A topic or subject-related film or recording
- Devices to view the film or recording as homework
- Paper and pens (or electronic devices) for noting down the summary and question

# Advantages

- Enables access to materials you may not have access to (e.g. looking at equipment and resources online)
- It promotes learner-centered activities and problem solving
- It can be more efficient for the organisation and learners (courses can be delivered in a shorter time frame)
- Enables discussions to take place during the session based on what has been learnt outside of the session

# Disadvantages

- Planning and marking can be time-consuming
- Requires learners to be self-motivated
- Learners will need a suitable device and/or internet connection to view the material
- Not all learners will engage with the concept and some may fall behind if they don't do it
- Increases screen time for learners who may already have high computer use such as social media access

# How can I measure my learners' progress, meet individual needs and demonstrate stretch and challenge for all?

Reading the learners' summaries will help you identify if they understood all of the material, part of the material or none of the material. The question they ask at the end of their summary will also give you an understanding of the knowledge they have gained.

The small and whole group discussions, when learners share their summaries and questions, will enable you to watch and listen to the conversations and resulting learning taking place.

To enable learners to demonstrate that they have been stretched and challenged, additional questions or tasks could be individually set based on the outcome of the summary and question, e.g. a research activity or a practical task.

---

### Tip

To help learners to format their notes and formulate a summary, you could design a template with relevant headings for them to address.

---

# Further reading and weblinks

FLIP Learning – *5 reasons why I love the WSQ Method* – https://tinyurl.com/yanpbhav

KQED Education – *Watch-think-write and other proven strategies for using video in the classroom* – https://tinyurl.com/ycysdvbf

# 48   Whip-round

| Individual | | Small group | √ | Large group | √ |
|---|---|---|---|---|---|
| Formative | √ | Summative | √ | Preparation time | 5 minutes |
| Informal | √ | Formal | √ | Timing | 5–10 minutes |
| British Values | * | Employability | * | After session marking? | |
| English | √ | Maths | * | Digital skills | * |
| Entry Level | √ | Level 1 and 2 | √ | Level 3 upwards | √ |

*depends upon what and how you are planning to use the approach*

## What is it?

A whip-round involves learners (on their own) having two minutes to think of, and write down in list form, as many facts as they can. These should be related to an open question you have posed regarding the current topic or subject.

All learners should stand up after the two minutes and take a turn to state one of their facts. Once a learner has stated their fact they can sit down.

Learners should cross the stated facts off their own list if they are the same or similar to the ones already stated. If all of their list has been crossed off, they should be given a minute to think of a new fact.

Once all of the learners are sat down, they can share with the group any facts not crossed off their lists. You will need to facilitate this by asking who has a fact which has not been stated.

A short group discussion should be held after the activity to review and summarise the question, topic or subject.

## What can it be used for?

A whip-round can be used as an initial assessment to ascertain each learner's knowledge and understanding. This could be prior to delivering a topic or a subject, and will help support you to identify any gaps in learning.

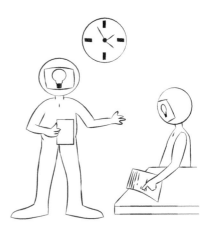

It can be used as a formal check on learning part way through a session, or to re-engage individuals. It can also be used at the end of a session as a closing activity to check learners' knowledge and understanding.

## Resources

- Paper and pens (or electronic devices) for noting down findings and ideas

## Advantages

👍 Quick and easy to set up with very little preparation time

👍 Good indicator to identify any gaps in learning

👍 Involves all learners

## Disadvantages

👎 Not all learners will want to engage with the activity

# How can I measure my learners' progress, meet individual needs and demonstrate stretch and challenge for all?

The fact each learner states will support you in identifying any gaps in their learning. It will also help to plan how you are going to meet any individual needs and measure progress.

When a learner states their fact, you could ask a direct question which is relevant to them. This will support individuals to demonstrate stretch and challenge by the differentiated question asked. For example, in a Countryside Management group the learners are identifying working dogs and their uses. A learner might state that an English Springer Spaniel has a double coat. A relevant directed question could be 'How does the double coat aid the spaniel to do its job?'. By answering the question, the learner is demonstrating their knowledge and understanding.

---

### Tip

Any identified gaps in learning should be revisited in future sessions. You may find it useful to keep notes regarding each learner.

---

## Further reading and weblinks

Professional Learning Board – https://tinyurl.com/jzuhxhu

The Teachers Tool Kit – https://tinyurl.com/oatnabf

# 49    Who wants to be a millionaire?

| Individual | | Small group | √ | Large group | √ |
|---|---|---|---|---|---|
| Formative | √ | Summative | √ | Preparation time | 30 minutes plus |
| Informal | √ | Formal | | Timing | 20–30 minutes |
| British Values | * | Employability | * | After session marking? | |
| English | √ | Maths | * | Digital skills | * |
| Entry Level | √ | Level 1 and 2 | √ | Level 3 upwards | √ |

*depends upon what and how you are planning to use the approach*

## What is it?

Who wants to be a millionaire is a quiz game originally designed to be played on a smart-board with the use of electronic voting devices (EVD).

Each learner is given an EVD and takes turns in answering multi-choice questions related to a topic or subject, by selecting one of four possible answers. It is similar to the popular television series.

Learners have three lifelines:

*   50:50 – where two out of the four answers are taken away
*   ask the audience – where learners can ask their peers using their EVD to vote on how they would answer
*   ask a friend – where a learner can select one peer to give their answer to the question (which can be accepted or not).

The aim of the game is to answer 15 questions correctly to win an imaginary million pounds. You can choose how much money is attributed to each question but the value should progressively increase. If a learner answers a question incorrectly, they are out of the game and the next learner takes a turn. The winner is the learner with the most money.

Alternatively, if you don't have access to EVDs, the activity can be played by the whole group at the same time. Questions can be asked verbally or you could design a PowerPoint presentation with multi-choice questions. Instead of giving three lifelines, learners can have three lives (one wrong question deducts one life), and scores can be tracked and noted on flipchart paper or a whiteboard.

# What can it be used for?

This activity has many uses, e.g. it can be used to prepare learners to undertake multi-choice tests or as a revision activity prior to an exam. It could be used as a recap from a previous session or at the end of a session as a closing activity. It can be an informal quiz during a session to refresh and re-engage learners and check their progress.

It's a great tool for correcting multi-choice homework, or as an extension activity with the whole group. If you are not using the electronic version, learners could be asked to take turns to act as record keeper to develop their maths skills.

# Resources

- A good reliable internet connection (if using electronic version)
- Electronic voting devices (if using electronic version)
- An interactive whiteboard (if using electronic version)
- Whiteboard or flipchart paper and pens (if using paper or PowerPoint version)
- Projector and computer device (if using paper or PowerPoint version)

# Advantages

👍 No electronic account or login by the learners is required

👍 It's engaging and supports social learning

👍 It's free to use

👍 Can make learning fun

👍 Great for learners who are usually unwilling to participate in group work

# Disadvantages

👎 Reliance on an internet connection (if using electronic version)

👎 Learners need an EVD to participate (if using electronic version)

👎 Time-consuming to create the questions and answers, and to set up

👎 Can cause too much competitiveness

👎 Can seem trivial to some learners

# How can I measure my learners' progress, meet individual needs and demonstrate stretch and challenge for all?

Individual progress is naturally demonstrated by learners answering the multi-choice questions correctly. As the learners progress, the questions should become harder which will stretch and challenge individuals. The first four questions should be relatively easy to give learners confidence and enable all learners to at least answer some questions correctly. The next few questions should be progressive, and the last five questions should be very hard to ensure the most knowledgeable learners are fully challenged.

You will need to plan the order of learners to take part, so that the most knowledgeable are left until later in the game.

An alternative method is to have one learner (in turn) go to the front of the room to answer the question. All the other learners should write down their answer on a large sheet of paper. They should hold these up after the question has been answered, for you to see. This helps you check individual knowledge.

> ### Tip
>
> Offer a small prize for the winner to further engage learners and encourage some competitiveness.

## Further reading and weblinks

Hertfordshire Grid for Learning – voting system – https://tinyurl.com/ycar7obx

One Stop English – how to use the activity – https://tinyurl.com/ycc27sty

Super Teachers Tool Home – free who wants to be a millionaire review game (electronic version) – https://tinyurl.com/y8xc8t7y

YouTube video – how to use this activity – https://tinyurl.com/y77z44e5

# 50 Worksheet

| Individual | √ | Small group | √ | Large group | √ |
|---|---|---|---|---|---|
| Formative | √ | Summative | √ | Preparation time | 30 minutes plus |
| Informal | √ | Formal | √ | Timing | 20–60 minutes |
| British Values | * | Employability | * | After session marking? | √ |
| English | √ | Maths | * | Digital skills | * |
| Entry Level | √ | Level 1 and 2 | √ | Level 3 upwards | √ |

*depends upon what and how you are planning to use the approach

## What is it?

A worksheet is an interactive document (either paper based or electronic), which learners read, learn from and respond to.

You can develop your own worksheet to suit your subject and different groups of learners. Often you can download these free from the internet (just use an online search engine to look for your topic or subject) or you could design your own. You might like to share them with colleagues who teach the same subject.

The worksheet could be question based,, e.g. a list of ten open questions, or multi-choice questions where the learner has to select the correct answer. They could be designed for the learner to fill in missing blanks, e.g. paragraphs of text with key words missing for the learner to work out and fill in. The worksheet could also be a topic or subject-related crossword or a word search.

For entry level and level 1 learners, a list of the missing words can be added at the bottom of the worksheet to give as prompts (you could add a few extra words to add to the challenge).

Alternatively, it could be a practical activity where learners have to follow the instructions, either written or as step-by-step images, to complete a task.

Worksheets are not suited to all levels of learners, and should not be relied upon too much, as there is very little teacher–learner interaction.

## What can it be used for?

There are many different ways to use worksheets as teaching and learning activities. They are an ideal revision tool if learners have an assessment or exam to undertake. Worksheets are also a great activity to use part way through a session to re-focus learners. They can be used informally to formatively assess a learner's progress or starting point. Alternatively, they could be used formally as a summative assessment of a learner's progress. In addition, worksheets can be used as an extension activity or homework task.

A worksheet can also be used like a handout. It could provide information about a topic, with questions for learners to complete to check ongoing understanding. Completed examples could be given to learners for them to compare their responses to, or to discuss in pairs or small groups. This would reduce your time to assess their responses, but you should be available to ask and answer questions.

## Resources

- A pre-designed worksheet
- Paper and pens (or electronic devices) for noting down findings and ideas

## Advantages

👍 Enables learners to work at their own pace

👍 Learners can support each other and learn from each other

## Disadvantages

👎 Time-consuming to produce (but can be used for future learners)

👎 Individual support and supervision might be required

👎 Suitable worksheets might need to be produced to enable learners to work at their own pace at different levels

## How can I measure my learners' progress, meet individual needs and demonstrate stretch and challenge for all?

Producing worksheets for varying abilities will ensure you meet individual needs and that every learner is stretched and challenged at the right level and pace for them, e.g. you may have some learners identifying technical words in a word search, whereas others are completing a crossword by answering questions about the same words. Alternatively, you may have some learners writing down their answers to questions, whereas others are circling multi-choice answers.

Marking the learners' work will support you in measuring individual progress and planning what else learners need to do to progress further.

> **Tip**
>
> If you are producing your own worksheets, ask a colleague to proofread these prior to sharing with your learners. This is to ensure there are no spelling or typing errors, and that everything makes sense.

# Further reading and weblinks

Super Teacher Worksheets – https://tinyurl.com/y9f5ellc

The Corner Stone for Teachers – *Five ways to turn a worksheet into a collaborative critical-thinking activity* – https://tinyurl.com/y899hxwo

# Appendix

## Ideas for grouping and pairing learners

It's always useful to have an idea prior to using any activity, of how you will group your learners. Individuals often behave differently in a group situation from when they work with others in a paired situation. Group dynamics can change, e.g. when new learners start a course later than others, when the venue or seating arrangements alter, or if there are personality clashes between learners.

Knowledge of your learners will help you to decide if they have the maturity to group themselves or whether you need to do this. If it's the former, you might find the same learners group together each time, i.e. those they get along with. If it's the latter, you might like to decide who will work with whom to help learners work with everyone over time.

Try not to do anything that could be conceived as stereotyping, e.g. grouping males separately from females, or older learners separately from younger ones.

You may wish to put learners in certain groups for different reasons, e.g. for classroom management; to improve inappropriate behaviour; or to support a shy learner to become more confident. For peer learning, placing the more experienced/high skilled learners with the less experienced/lower skilled learners helps them to support and learn from each other.

It's fine to have some groups with more learners than others, as this can be addressed when another activity takes place. You might find it useful to keep a note of who has worked with whom over time.

The following table will give you a few ideas of activities you could use to group and pair your learners.

| Grouping or pairing activity | Large group | Small group | Same/ mixed skill level | Higher skill with lower skill | Random | Paired: differentiated | Paired: random | Classroom Management |
|---|---|---|---|---|---|---|---|---|
| Hand out different coloured cards or straws as the learners arrive. Learners match their colour to form a group. | ✓ | ✓ | ✓ | ✓ | | ✓ | | ✓ |
| Hand out sweets with different coloured wrappers. Learners match the wrappers to form a group. | | ✓ | ✓ | ✓ | | ✓ | | ✓ |
| Use letters of the alphabet on card and hand out to the learners. All the As form a group, all the Bs form a group etc. | ✓ | ✓ | ✓ | ✓ | | ✓ | | ✓ |
| Give out parts of a picture (choose a set number of parts for the number of learners you want to be in each group). Once the learners have found the matching pieces to their picture, they form a group. | | ✓ | ✓ | ✓ | | ✓ | | ✓ |
| Allocate numbers to each learner. Ask numbers one to six to form a group, seven to twelve, thirteen to eighteen etc. Change the numbers depending upon the group sizes you want. | ✓ | ✓ | ✓ | ✓ | | ✓ | | ✓ |
| Give out two halves of a sentence related to the current topic, to different learners. Learners have to find the person who completes their sentence and pair up. | | | ✓ | ✓ | | ✓ | | |

| Grouping or pairing activity | Large group | Small group | Same/ mixed skill level | Higher skill with lower skill | Random | Paired: differentiated | Paired: random | Classroom Management |
|---|---|---|---|---|---|---|---|---|
| Using famous names, give out the first name to half of the learners and the surname to the other half. Learners must find their partner by matching the names. | | | ✓ | ✓ | | ✓ | | ✓ |
| Mix up several lengths of string. Each learner must grab one end of the string and see who they become attached to. | | | | | | | ✓ | |
| Display a seating plan which puts the learners in the most appropriate place. | ✓ | ✓ | ✓ | ✓ | | ✓ | | ✓ |
| Randomly take a wrapped sweet or piece of Lego out of a bag and group according to the colour. You will need to ensure you have enough different colours. | | ✓ | | | ✓ | | ✓ | |
| Select team captains and let them choose their team members. | ✓ | ✓ | | | ✓ | | ✓ | |
| Ask the learners to work with the person to their right/left/behind or in front of them. | ✓ | ✓ | | | ✓ | ✓ | ✓ | |

# Index